There are those among us who take our practice of yoga, and yet they can holding in your hands begins to build a bridge between these worlds and to offer some of the timeless wisdom that unites them both. In a time of much intolerance, *Yogadevotion* reminds us of the importance of keeping our hearts, minds, and bodies open and our breath steady and prayerful.

DEBORAH ADELE
Author, *The Yamas & Niyamas: Exploring Yoga's Ethical Practice*

As a Christian pastor and a new practitioner of yoga, Pastor Senarighi's work is invaluable in helping me meld my faith tradition into my practice of yoga. I highly recommend *Yogadevotion*!

JOHN HOGENSON
Former Senior Pastor, Mount Olivet Lutheran Church

I was fortunate to be Heidi Green's medical oncologist while she was undergoing therapy for her breast cancer. As all of us know, there are many pathways to better health. Medical therapy is important, but spiritual therapy also plays a major role. Heidi found yoga to be a very useful component of her breast cancer treatment, and I give her a lot of credit for co-writing *Yogadevotion* to share what she learned as a way to help others.

DOUGLAS YEE, MD
Director, Masonic Cancer Center, University of Minnesota

This book is a welcome and creative contribution to a societal matrix in which yoga has gone mainstream while church congregations are diminishing. With insightful reflections on Scripture, this wide-ranging approach to spiritual practice guides us into a faith-based experience of yoga as one way of leading people to an experience of the Holy. Cindy and Heidi invite us to combine praise of God with our posture practice, and to come home to our bodies by practicing Presence. *Yogadevotion* offers a faith-based yoga practice accessible to all who cultivate encounters with God both on the mat and in one's daily living. A timely gift, indeed!

THOMAS RYAN, CSP
Director, Paulist Fathers Office for Ecumenical and Interfaith Relations
Author, *Prayer of Heart and Body: Meditation and Yoga as Christian Spiritual Practice*

Yoga is union. It invites union of breath, body, mind, and spirit. No matter what age, health condition, belief system, or physical abilities we have, yoga is a gift of being present in that union. As a lifelong spiritual seeker, my Catholic upbringing often seemed to be in conflict with my yoga journey. I no longer feel that way. For I know that the search for peace that surpasses all understanding is what unites us. *Yogadevotion*'s weekly lessons offer an amazing tool that invite us to feel the presence of mind, body, spirit, and God. I looked forward to each devotion and yoga treasure like a cup of soothing tea for my body and soul.

SHERRY ZAK MORRIS
CEO, Yoga Journey Productions and co-founder
of the Yoga Vista Academy

When I was a boy, I was taught to pray by folding my hands and bowing my head. That was a good start, but there are so many other ways we can work with our bodies to open our hearts to God, to life, and to love. *Yogadevotion* will introduce you to fifty-two of those ways, one for each week of the year. Thoughtful meditations are linked with beautiful photographs and simple instructions. I can think of so many friends who will love this book!

BRIAN MCLAREN
Author, *We Make the Road by Walking: A Year-Long Quest
for Spiritual Formation, Reorientation, and Activation*

Yogadevotion shows how yoga, properly understood, goes beyond the physical to engage all we are: body, mind, and spirit. This marvelous book is a bridge between the yoga mat and the spiritual experience of transcendence. I am sure the ancient sages who introduced yoga would smile in approval of these insights.

LARRY DOSSEY, MD
Author, *One Mind: How Our Individual Mind
Is Part of a Greater Consciousness and Why It Matters*

YOGADEVOTION

YOGADEVOTION

PRACTICING
IN THE
PRESENCE

CINDY SENARIGHI AND **HEIDI GREEN**

With deep gratitude

for our Creator's love

and the support of our

teachers, students, and friends

who have accompanied us

on this journey,

WE DEDICATE THIS BOOK

TO OUR FAMILIES.

Contents

CHAPTER 1

Why Practice Faith-Based Yoga?

Chronic stress, cancer, heart disease, arthritis, eating disorders, and addiction— these are just some of the conditions in our Western world for which medical doctors are recommending yoga.[1] And Americans are listening. It's estimated that approximately 20 million people,[2] 8% of the adult population, are taking yoga classes in the United States annually. Yet in an effort to present a class accessible to the widest audience, most American yoga instructors today avoid teaching devotional yoga practices such as reading sacred text, meditation, and prayer and pay only perfunctory attention to breath work—all keystone practices of traditional yoga that offer the most healing and spiritual growth opportunities.[3]

Classical yoga was centered on devotional practices, presented in ancient Sanskrit, the language of the time. The modern use of Sanskrit in describing yoga practices unfortunately seems to have created the misunderstanding that devotional yoga practices are derived from Hinduism. In fact, the opposite is true: yoga predates Hinduism by many centuries.[4] Because of a general lack of public understanding about the classical roots of yoga, many American yoga teachers, and their employers and students, fear yoga being

---

1   The National Institute of Health website states that yoga is one of the "top 10 complementary health approaches" and lists a variety of studies and current research on yoga and health: https://nccih.nih.gov/health/yoga .

2   Yoga in America Market Study, http://www.yogajournal.com/article/press-releases/ yoga-journal-releases-2012-yoga-in-america-market-study/ .

3   *Asana* (physical pose) is only one of the eight limbs of yoga, yet most Western yoga classes offer only *Asana* practice. The other limbs are *Yama* (ethics and integrity), *Niyama* (self-discipline and spiritual observances), *Pranayama* (breath control), *Pratyahara* (sensory control), *Dharana* (concentration and inner awareness), *Dhyana* (devotion and meditation on the divine), and *Samadhi* (union with the divine). See Swami Satchindanada, *The Yoga Sutras of Patanjali* (Yogaville, VA: Integral Yoga Publications, 2012).

4   It is difficult to date Hinduism as it has no founder and no central doctrine. It is commonly believed to have developed on the Indian Continent in the Vedic Period, around 500 BCE, from an assortment of indigenous religions. Yoga is believed to be much older. Yoga appears in the ancient text, the Rigveda, dating to 1500-1200 BCE; some scholars date yoga to 5,000 BCE.

labeled an Eastern religion and therefore strip devotional techniques from their instruction, as they are unable or unwilling to show students how to incorporate their own faith traditions into their yoga practice.

The contemplative practice of meditation seems to have escaped these religious misunderstandings often associated with yoga, in part because meditation techniques are taught using modern language and because sacred movement was largely lost as a contemplative practice in Christianity during the Reformation, while meditative practices continued. Similar to meditation, yoga is just another contemplative technique and as such may be practiced with or without a faith component. Most important, yoga, like meditation, may be practiced as a way to expand our *own* faith practices.

Western medical research shows time and again that the safe practice of yoga has health benefits, not the least of which is an ability to address issues that can cause disease (dis-ease) and stress. The practice of yoga strengthens our body, calms our central nervous system, and filters and settles our thoughts—thoughts that can clutter our mind and wreak havoc in our body. As a result, yoga has become widely accepted as a complementary therapy, part of an integrated treatment plan to manage or recover from illness, with the goal of seeking cure.[5]

Healing, however, is more complex. Healing in faith language is promised whether or not cure takes place. To heal is to make whole. These bodies we inhabit are temporary, and there are certain circumstances, like pain, suffering, and broken relationships, that simply do not make sense. We seek wholeness that is outside our ability to provide for ourselves. When our mind quiets, a window opens that connects us to something greater than ourselves. When our mind quiets and we bring to that quiet our faith, we tap into the infinite goodness of God, within which we experience wholeness. This is the true source of yoga's healing power.

In his research Dr. Herbert Benson from Harvard University Medical School found that belief, our faith life, is a powerful force in healing the body.[6] According to Benson, biologically we are "wired for God." By removing devotional practices from our yoga classes we extract much of the power from the practice, with little increase in benefit beyond that of a traditional exercise or relaxation class. If Western yoga students want to truly experience the profound healing, mental, and spiritual-growth effects of yoga, they would benefit from learning how to incorporate into their pose-based (*asana*) yoga practice the devotional yoga components of studying sacred text, meditation, and prayer from their own faith traditions and beliefs.

---

5   The definition of cure is recovery from disease.
6   Herbert Benson, *Timeless Healing* (Simon & Schuster, 1997).

We have written this book to show others how to incorporate their faith traditions into a yoga practice. Our faith tradition is Christian, but the formula is the same for applying your own faith to a devotional yoga practice: study of sacred text, reflection on application to the world in which we live, meditation, prayer, breath work, and gentle movement. Both of us have experienced the healing power of yoga and have grown in our relationship to God through yoga. Our yoga practice is at times mundane and occasionally profound, but what makes all the difference is the discipline of the *practice*—setting aside a time each day to open ourselves to God's presence. We hope our readers will be inspired by our devotions to practice faith-based yoga and to share with others the love of God that they experience in Yogadevotion.

Cindy's Faith-Yoga Story

In the mid to late 1990s yoga experienced a revival in the United States by being reinvented as another way to work out. Yoga had gained a foothold among American young adults in the late 1960s (along with interest in Eastern philosophies and alternative lifestyles), but the renewed interest in the 1990s came through what some have called the "back door" of fitness instruction. While many of us were sweating it out in aerobics classes, companies like YogaFit® and Baptiste Yoga™ were training fitness instructors in the benefits of teaching yoga. I approached my first yoga class as a fitness instructor who was also a registered psychiatric nurse, believing that if I learned to teach yoga I could stay in the industry when I was too old to teach anything else. As I look back, the day I stepped into my first yoga class was the beginning of a beautiful and God-breathed transformation from a type A, overworked, stressed-out achiever to someone who seeks comfort in the stillness and presence of God.

God was not on my mind when I took my first yoga training. But during that initial experience, while in a restorative yoga pose, I found myself to be alert and calm, with an overwhelming sense of God's Presence. The sensation was like nothing I had ever felt before. I experienced a sense of warmth, love, and peace, as though God were saying *"I have been waiting for you to notice I'm here and that I love you."* That evening I had dinner with the friend who had arranged the training and told her what had happened. She too had experienced a connection she had not felt before. Agreeing that people of faith and those seeking spiritual growth would be excited to share this experience, we started teaching physical yoga classes with faith-based language in a devotional format to invite the experience of God's healing presence. We called it Yogadevotion.

Beware! When God shows up unexpectedly in your life you become aware of things in a new way. Two life-changers happened shortly after my first yoga instructor training, both of which opened my eyes to a need for more of the healing presence I had experienced: I became a parish nurse and entered seminary. As a parish nurse I came to see suffering from a different perspective than I had as a psychiatric nurse. The pain and brokenness I was witnessing introduced to me some burning God questions.

We all have our issues; we all have experienced in some form or another the brokenness in our bodies and in our relationships. Through faith-based yoga I have been able to reclaim my inner connection to God and to find answers concerning the pain and brokenness in my own life, as well as in the lives of those with whom I have connected through my work. For Christians like me this understanding comes through the healing life and ministry of Jesus. But here is the really cool thing: it doesn't matter whether we "get it." God shows up in our lives and on our mats whether or not we understand God. God's activity in our lives and in the world cannot be restrained by our inability to comprehend what God is up to. The physical practice of yoga is a vehicle to a healthy mind and body, but I have found that devotional yoga opens us up to experiencing God's Presence in body, mind, and spirit. My personal yoga instructor said it best:

Yoga was never intended to be separate from devotion to God. The physical practice is to settle our bodies so we can sit with our breath, enjoy the healing Presence, and be connected in our relationship to God and each other. Union of body, mind, and spirit has always been the intended outcome of yoga practice.

As Yogadevotion grew, so did my sense of a calling to ordained ministry. Years later I came to see my ministry as a path where passion—for God, yoga, and healing— meets the needs of the world. Devotional yoga opens our eyes to areas in which God is active in the world and guides the process of healing and connection to the Creator and to each other. I hope that you too will experience God's healing love as you bring your faith traditions to your mat—as you *Practice in the Presence*.

Heidi's Faith-Yoga Story

I came to yoga more than 40 years ago when I was a teenager in the 1970s. The Vietnam War was coming to an end, and the Beatles had just broken up, to my great dismay. This was the time of the musicals *Godspell* and *Jesus Christ Superstar*, long hair and tie-dyed shirts. I wanted my dad to stop smoking and had heard that yoga could be helpful. So he and I enrolled in a class. This was back before the secular "studio" culture of yoga sprang up, so those early classes were marked by lots of chanting, incense, and inverted postures. My first yoga teacher had been trained in India and practiced Integral Yoga, a yoga lineage friendly to Christianity and famous for promoting the slogan "Truth is one, paths are many." Having both a wise yoga instructor and a family that supported both my Christian faith and my yoga practice, I never felt any conflict between the two.

As the years passed I practiced yoga on a regular basis. From Integral Yoga I moved on to practicing Iyengar for many years. And somewhere along the way I added meditation to my practice. Even though I had now been studying for decades, I never considered myself "good enough" to teach yoga. The secular studio culture of the 1990s introduced an athletic component to the practice, of which I felt I had nothing to contribute. So I continued along with my countercultural, "old school" yoga practice, taking the occasional class and practicing daily to help keep me happy and sane.

Then one day a bombshell hit. In my early 50s I was diagnosed with breast cancer. My mother had died in her 50s of an especially aggressive type of breast cancer, so I was very frightened. Four factors helped me through cancer treatment: my faith; the love of family and friends, including my church community; a great medical team at the University of Minnesota Masonic Cancer Center; and yoga. I practiced *every day* through my cancer treatment—even if only for ten minutes. And something magical happened. I began to feel better. And I became aware of God's Presence, in a real-life, *Am I hallucinating?* kind of way. Every time I got on my mat, every time I paused to take a deep, slow breath I felt God's Presence in the form of Jesus, reassuring me, "*I'm right here. I'm walking with you on this journey.*"

I am five years out from my original cancer diagnosis—and cancer free. I look back on my cancer experience now as a kind of blessing, for it was during treatment that I learned that God's Presence is real, something that can be *experienced*. And I learned that all my years of engaging in contemplative practices, particularly devotional yoga, had provided me with the tools to experience God's healing Presence when I needed it most.

I now had something to share about my faith and yoga. Encouraged by Cindy, I got my yoga teaching certification, and started instructing for Yogadevotion. I began studying Vini (therapeutic) yoga. At the same time I undertook and completed a four-year program for lay ministry in the Episcopal Church and discerned that I was called to a healing lay ministry. I pray that our book will encourage others to practice devotional yoga and will lead them, too, to experience the ever-present, healing Presence that has so blessed me. Peace be with you! *Namaste.*

CHAPTER 2

How to Use the Weekly Devotions

Devotional yoga may be integrated into any pose-oriented, *asana*, yoga discipline. We have successfully integrated our devotions into such diverse practices as Yin Yoga, Chair Yoga (for those unable to do yoga from the floor), Restorative Yoga, Yoga for Cancer, Yoga for Arthritis, Soma Yoga, and even a Power or Strength Yoga class! Our most common class, however, is *vinyasa* or gentle-flow yoga.

We assume our readers already practice yoga, as this is a book not about how to practice yoga poses (*asana*) but how to integrate your faith traditions into your yoga practice.

For easy reference we are providing in Appendix A, in the back of the book, a cross-referenced list of yoga poses that we name in the weekly practices, referring to both their common English and their Sanskrit names. We hope this makes the poses easy to research if you are unfamiliar with or desire to review a named pose.

Each of our weekly practices is organized into five sections:

- Scripture from sacred text;
- Spiritual Focus from a non-Scripture quotation;
- Devotion, a reflection on the Scripture and Spiritual Focus;
- Breath Prayer that captures the essence of the practice; and a
- Pose Focus to embody the practice.

We consider these devotional elements the basics and are confident that once you have established your own devotional yoga practice, other devotional practices, based on your own needs and spiritual traditions, will follow.

It is not necessary to follow the weekly devotions in order—although we have organized them according to the calendar year, and they may be generally applied to a liturgical calendar. We use the Revised Common Lectionary to inform our Scripture selections. See Appendix C, "Adapting the Devotions to a Liturgical Calendar." In addition, we have included in Appendix B an alphabetical index of the Weekly Practices; this may be used to find a devotional practice that addresses your current or particular needs.

SCRIPTURE—Each week's devotion is based on a passage from sacred text. We strongly believe that the study of sacred text is essential for a devotional practice. The yoga observance or *niyama* of *syadhyaya* encourages this. Our own religious backgrounds are in mainstream Christian churches, so we gravitate toward the sacred texts of the Old Testament (Hebrew Bible) and the New Testament that are included in this book. But we also believe that sacred texts from many other religions and spiritual traditions may be used in devotional yoga. We encourage our students to study the sacred texts that are most relevant to them and to their personal connection with the Creator.

SPIRITUAL FOCUS—The Spiritual Focus is a non-Scripture quotation, secular in nature that affirms the practice. Often it provides a colloquial "translation" or some clarification of the Scripture that it follows and, as such, may sometimes be more readily accessible than the Scripture.

DEVOTION—The Devotion is the reflection on the Scripture and Spiritual Focus of each week's practice. In the Devotion the sacred text is examined for insight into our lives today, in this world. The Devotion is meant to inspire your own reflection on the meaning of the week's practice and to provide "food for thought" on how the message can move out of our heads and into our daily actions beyond our yoga mats.

BREATH PRAYER—We practice breath-centered yoga. Simply put, this means that the movement in our practice begins and ends with a breath. Breath is the key to linking body, mind, and spirit. We orient ourselves throughout our practice with a Breath Prayer, which distills the essence of the practice into just a few words. Using the Breath Prayer throughout our practice keeps us grounded and is particularly useful when our attention is wandering. Many of the Breath Prayers in this book begin with I AM. This is God's name as told to Moses in Exodus 3:14. We use I AM in the Breath Prayer to honor God. A Sacred Word (see below) may be substituted for the Breath Prayer at your discretion. Either technique helps us reaffirm our commitment to stay present throughout the practice.

POSE FOCUS—The Pose Focus is selected to embody the weekly practice theme and *is a suggestion only*. Listening to the teacher within, our only physical yoga goal is to find steadiness and comfort in each *asana*. If it is accessible, the suggested Pose Focus might be the apex pose for your practice, or it may give you an idea of how another pose, more readily available to you, might embody the spirit of the practice.

Each student needs to be mindful of his or her body's limitations and modify *asana*, their physical yoga practice, in a manner that will ensure comfort and safety in each posture. If you are new to yoga, we highly recommend that you first seek instruction from a Yoga Alliance[1] certified yoga instructor and check with your doctor for verification that a physical yoga practice is safe for your body.

Sacred Word

We encourage students to search for and find their own Sacred Word or *mantra* to be used in yoga practice. The student repeats the sacred word, coordinating it with the breath, to focus the mind and calm the body. A sacred word or mantra is used in many styles of meditation. In some contemplative Christian traditions a personal sacred word is used as a conduit to Centering Prayer. Here are a few suggestions for a personal sacred word:

Amen	God	Grace
Gratitude	Heal	Jesu
Peace	Yahweh	Shalom

We offer no particular direction in our devotions for the use of a sacred word. In our practice our sacred word is our safety net—that to which we return when nothing else seems to be "working." We repeat our sacred word to ourselves to reconnect with our breath, to focus our minds, and to return us to the present. We also repeat our sacred word when the week's Breath Prayer or Devotion isn't what we need, or when we can't practice—or don't want to practice—perhaps when we are frustrated or bored with our practice. We use our sacred word to cocoon our thoughts in meditation and to bring us to the stillness we need in order to experience God's presence. But mostly we use our sacred word to affirm our connection to the Creator.

---

1   Yoga Alliance is the main certifying body of yoga instructors in the United States. You may find Yoga Alliance certified instructors on their website: https://www.yogaalliance.org/.

CHAPTER 3

The Devotions

The Practice of Freshening Up

SCRIPTURE So we're not giving up. How could we! Even though on the outside it often looks like things are falling apart on us, on the inside, where God is making new life, not a day goes by without God's unfolding grace.

2 CORINTHIANS 4:16 *THE MESSAGE*

SPIRITUAL FOCUS "Live as if you were to die tomorrow, learn as if you were to live forever."

MAHATMA GANDHI

DEVOTION During the Great Depression bathing was a luxury. The phrase *"don't throw the baby out with the bath water"* was born out of the practice of family members sharing the same bath water. Since the babies were last to bathe . . . well, you get the idea. Because of the high value placed on water for bathing, the value of freshening up was understood. Freshening up was a way of preserving water while still coming out feeling clean and renewed. Today freshening up is a way of identifying what is still usable and good—as well as what has served its purpose and we may let go.

In the New Year we encounter many invitations to let go of the old and usher in the new. A subtle variation occurs when, while honoring the old ways that have served us well, we recognize the kind of newness that will improve our quality of life. In this continuum of transformation we find balance: we can embrace the new without fixating upon or regretting the loss of the old. The newness spoken of in our scripture is found in God's unfolding grace; this newness to which we are drawn constitutes a "freshening up" of what God has done and continues to do. In yoga we often encourage participants to let go of what no longer serves them. There are some old ways of thinking about life, faith, and relationships (even yoga) that have worked for us in the past but need at this point to be put aside. We honor what God has done in our lives and lean in to God's continuing grace as it unfolds, new and fresh for this day.

BREATH PRAYER

Inhale ◆ I Am

Exhale ◆ Refreshed

POSE FOCUS Knees to Chest pose, *apanasana,* lengthens the lower back muscles as light pressure is put on the belly. It brings blood flow to the lower torso and abdominal organs, encouraging the release of blockages. Begin on your back or in a chair and on exhalation gently squeeze your abdominal muscles as you bring one or both knees toward your chest. On inhalation return to your starting position with neutral spine. Repeat for three to six cycles of breath before holding the pose, knee(s) to chest, if it serves your body. If not, let it go.

The Practice of the Road Less Traveled

SCRIPTURE And having been warned in a dream not to return to Herod, they left for their own country by another road.

MATTHEW 2:12

SPIRITUAL FOCUS "Two roads diverged in a wood, and I, I took the one less traveled by. And that has made all the difference."

ROBERT FROST

DEVOTION There are several interesting twists to the story of the Magi, the so-called "three kings." The Magi are astronomers, guided by a star. They express great joy at their discovery of the baby Jesus and bring gifts befitting a king. The Magi are not Jewish or believers in God; they are those *other*, those uninitiated and unentitled ones from afar. And yet God reveals to these "others" the light of the world, the Christ Child. The Magi in meeting the Christ Child are changed: some translations say they are "enlightened." And, so changed, they hear (and heed) the warning "in a dream" to return home by a *different* road.

One might say that an encounter with the living God changes every-thing. A new path appears, a new direction accompanied by God's prom-ised presence. When we come to our yoga practice with the openness our faith inspires we invite that encounter. We might practice an *asana*, a new breath technique or modification of a pose, and suddenly find that our awareness opens to the presence and promptings of the inner Spirit of God. This awareness has the power to change the course of our lives. God not only promises us these little life-changing epiphanies but guides us toward them. When we practice our faith, both on and off of our mats, we become more aware of that *different* road to which God may be leading us. It is a road less traveled but one that leads to life and love with the One who created us for the journey.

BREATH PRAYER

Inhale ◆ I Am

Exhale ◆ Aware

POSE FOCUS Mindfulness is a contemplative practice that draws our attention to the present. Practicing mindfulness is more difficult than it sounds, as our busy minds are constantly ping-ponging between the past, present, and future. One way to cultivate mindfulness—we might call it *presence* in the *present*—is to intentionally exercise awareness. In your practice this week focus your complete attention on one favorite pose. To help keep your busy mind present, ask questions of the pose: *Where do I feel tightness? Where do I feel loose? Where do I feel warmth? Where do I feel cool? Where do I feel comfort? Where do I feel discomfort?* Observe. Be present. And don't be surprised if a new path forward emerges.

The Practice of Listening
to our Internal Teacher, the Soul

SCRIPTURE The law of the LORD is perfect, reviving the soul.
PSALM 19:7

SPIRITUAL FOCUS "Belief consists in accepting the affirmations of the soul; unbelief, in denying them."
RALPH WALDO EMERSON

DEVOTION One of our most powerful experiences as a yoga student comes when we learn to listen to our body. In listening to our body we learn what the body needs or doesn't need, on and off the mat. In listening to our body we take responsibility for adjusting and adapting our breath and our *asana*, for the greatest benefit in our practice. Learning to listen to our body is a foundation for learning to listen to our soul, to the spirit of God within. When we listen deeply, deliberately attuning ourselves to incoming affirmations, we are taught and experience the healing power of God's love.

The companion gospel story to today's psalm is that of Jesus teaching and proclaiming that the Spirit of the Lord was upon him, that he was indeed the anointed one. Although the priests and people in the synagogue did not believe his teaching, their skepticism did not stop him from proclaiming that he had come to bring healing to all people. As people of faith we too are anointed. When we practice listening to our body and Spirit, the internal teacher, our faith is affirmed. In creating space for God to be present in our lives we are made whole: our soul is revived. When we take our revived souls off the mat into our everyday life, we bring healing to all of God's children.

BREATH PRAYER

Inhale ◆ I Am

Exhale ◆ Listening

POSE FOCUS It is difficult to listen to our soul when we are stressed. Legs Up the Wall, *viparita karani*, is a mild inversion that is celebrated for bringing serenity back to our spirit. There are many variations of Legs Up the Wall, but no matter the variation a principle applies: *less is more*. Add your favorite version of Legs Up the Wall into your practice this week. When in the pose ask yourself *Of what can I let go?* Make adjustments as needed. Then come into stillness and listen.

The Practice of Being Light

SCRIPTURE If we walk in the light as he himself is in the light, we have fellowship with one another.

1 JOHN 1:7

SPIRITUAL FOCUS "When you look at electrical things you can see that they are made of small and big wires, cheap and expensive all lined up. Until the current runs through them there will be no light. Those wires are you and me and the current is God. We have the power to let the current pass through us, use us and produce the light of the world or we can refuse to be used and allow darkness to spread."

MOTHER TERESA

DEVOTION It was a gloomy, rainy winter afternoon. I climbed the stairs to the yoga studio and sank with a rather lackluster demeanor onto my mat. The whole class seemed to be in a funk, and the teacher, reading the energy level in the room, said, *"Just because you can't see the sunshine, don't be fooled; you know that the sun is there. The light of the sun cannot be overcome by the darkness of the rain."* Sound familiar? Recall the verse just prior to this week's Scripture quotation: *"The life was the light of all people. The light shines in the darkness, and the darkness did not overcome it"* (John 1:4–5).

The theme of light and darkness is one in which we rest this time of year—and how appropriate. Just a short time ago during the shortest day of the year, with the least amount of daylight, we celebrated in darkness the birth of the Light, Jesus, God in human form. The darkness of this world cannot extinguish *this* Light. That is Good News for us, as there may be times when, try as we may, we can't distinguish the Son through the murky atmosphere. What a gift it is that our relationship with God is independent of our ability to see the light. In fact, our faith teaches that, through grace, the Light already resides *within* each of us. When we practice our faith, regardless of those at times deceptive outward circumstances, the Light in us grows and reflects on those around us.

On and off of the mat . . . be Light.

BREATH PRAYER

Inhale ◆ I Am

Exhale ◆ Light

POSE FOCUS Incorporate an extra side stretch into your practice this week, and bring your attention to the contrasting movement of elongation on one side of the rib cage against the contraction of the opposite side. Reverse Warrior pose, *viparita virabhadrasana,* is a favorite side stretch used in many *vinyasa* sequences. Begin in Warrior II, turn your front hand palm upward, and drop your back hand to your leg. With breath, lift your front arm to the heavens, enjoying a side bend toward the back of the mat. Breathe into your torso God's white, healing light, and experience openness above constriction—lightness above darkness. Lift and be light.

The Practice of Removing our Mask

SCRIPTURE Moses did not know that the skin of his face shone because he had been talking with God. When Aaron and all the Israelites saw Moses, the skin of his face was shining, and they were afraid to come near him. . . When Moses had finished speaking with them, he put a veil on his face. . . . [W]henever Moses went in before the LORD to speak with him, he would take the veil off, until he came out . . . [T]he Israelites would see the face of Moses, that the skin of his face was shining; and Moses would put the veil on his face again.

EXODUS 34:29–35

SPIRITUAL FOCUS "I have the immense joy of being a man, a member of a race in which God Himself became incarnate. . . . And if only everybody could realize this! But it cannot be explained. There is no way of telling people that they are all walking around shining like the sun."

THOMAS MERTON

DEVOTION In the early 1990s a yogi named Baron Baptiste, born of American yogi parents, began to explore the power of yoga to transform people's lives. In 2002 he published a book titled *Journey into Power,* in which he shared his own transformational experience, as well as those of some students. One of the tenets of his teaching was that we wear masks that become obstacles to our being transformed into who we truly are: spiritual beings.

We all at times hide behind masks, but when doing so becomes the norm we move from self-protection into self-denial mode. Moses, in this week's Scripture, found himself in the presence of God. Being in such close proximity to deity was so glorious that the radiance of God was seen by others after the fact as reflected light on Moses' face. In the Old Testament the glory of God was considered to be so brilliant that human beings could not look upon it safely, prompting Moses to temporarily don a veil or mask after emerging from God's presence.

Dropping our mask, hard as this is to do, is something we can practice both on and off our mat. In peaceful silence we open our hearts to trust God with all that we are as human beings: physical, emotional, and spiritual. We listen to the teachings that speak of God's full presence in the fully human, earthly Jesus. When it comes to our relationship with God, our need for that mask has been forever eradicated. We are invited into the story as spiritual beings engaged in a personal, human experience with Jesus—not just for our own sake but for the sake of the world into which God entered—for the sake of each other.

BREATH PRAYER

Inhale ◆ I

Exhale ◆ Am

POSE FOCUS Lion's Breath, *simhasana,* is a pose that ignites our inner fire, helping us conquer our fears. This is a powerful *pranayama*, so do Lion's Breath only near the end of your practice, when your body and mind are ready. Lion's Breath is often done in Hero's pose, but it can be done from any comfortable seat. Once you've found your seat inhale deeply, and with a *big* audible exhalation (emanating from the back of your throat) widen your eyes, open your mouth, drop your jaw, and stick out your tongue. Relax the face on inhalation. Try several rounds of Lion's Breath and then stop and observe the heat that was generated in the pose. Use this powerful energy to conquer your fears and remove your mask.

The Practice of Clear Vision

SCRIPTURE I have called you to live right and well. I have taken responsibility for you, kept you safe. I have set you among my people to bind them to me, and provided you as a lighthouse to the nations, to make a start at bringing people into the open, into the light: opening blind eyes.

ISAIAH 42:6–7 *THE MESSAGE*

SPIRITUAL FOCUS "Your eyes have the capacity to see Truth. When you look without judgment, without the interference of thought and mind, the eyes become the windows of God and you perceive the Truth."

VASANT LAD (DOCTOR OF AYURVEDIC MEDICINE)

DEVOTION As a chaplain in the local senior facility I had the privilege of knowing 103-year-old Pearl. Pearl was a woman of strong faith and opinion, whose greatest frustration was with her fading vision. On one of our visits Pearl shared her disappointment that the facility in which she lived paid lots of attention to Mardi Gras and not enough to Ash Wednesday, the day following. We engaged in conversation around these two events and landed on an agreement that we did not need to value one over the other: each offered a unique lens through which to perceive God's activity in the world. The next day, as I placed ashes on her forehead (a traditional Christian ritual to help us remember that we are claimed by God), Pearl looked up, smiled, and murmured, "*Dead to judgment, alive in Jesus.*" Pearl's physical ability to see had not improved, but her spiritual vision had become clearer when she chose to see through more than one lens.

Clear vision is not just an outcome of new information; it is accepting an invitation to see in a new light, to perceive things as God would have us see them. In yoga we open our eyes in balance; we focus our eye gaze or *drishti* on a single point, clearing our vision. We make eye contact with our neighbor as we share the peace. Looking outward allows us to see ourselves in community, in balance with our neighbor. At the beginning and end of each class we close our eyes and focus inward on the truth of what God sees: our true selves. Instead of hearing words of judgment or condemnation, instead of hearing "*You could have done better,*" we hear God's voice assuring us: "*You are mine. I love you just as you are.*"

If your faith journey includes Lenten observances, consider including the practice of clear vision. Be open to seeing God in each other in new ways: drop the judgment and live like Jesus. Let your eyes become the windows through which you catch sight of the truth of God's love.

BREATH PRAYER

Inhale ◆ Open

Exhale ◆ My Eyes

POSE FOCUS Our poor eyes get so tired. Laptops, smart phones, e-books, ipads, TVs: the list of devices in our everyday lives that strain our eyes seems to get longer every day. This week add some eye exercises into your practice. A favorite is to move your eyes as though your gaze were following the second hand of a clock. To begin, sit tall and come into your breath. Start your eye circles with a neutral centered gaze, and then take your gaze to 1 o'clock, 2 o'clock, 3 o'clock, etc. Circle all the way around to 12 o'clock and then return to a centered, soft gaze. Take a few slow breaths and then begin a counter-clockwise rotation of your gaze, starting at 12 o'clock and ending at 1 o'clock. Return again to a centered, soft gaze and close your eyes. Allow your eyes to relax into their sockets and smile into the darkness, assured that God will open your eyes.

The Practice of Inward Journey

SCRIPTURE We do not lose heart. Even though our outer nature is wasting away, our inner nature is being renewed day by day.
2 CORINTHIANS 4:16

SPIRITUAL FOCUS "The farther the outward journey takes you, the deeper the inward journey must be."
HENRI NOUWEN

DEVOTION The Reverend Gordon Crosby said in a 1989 sermon, "*Faith is trusting the flow, reveling in the view, carried beyond all existing boundaries.*" How we view boundaries has something to do with our personality type and may inform our spiritual journey. For an extrovert the inward journey may be a challenge because information about the self is more easily gathered and processed outwardly. For an introvert the inward journey may be more easily accessible but remains incomplete unless there is some outward expression of self—something an introvert may find challenging. Neither is better or worse; the journeys and their boundaries are simply different.

Reverend Gordon's words invite us to trust the flow of the journey and worry less about the boundaries. When we come to that place of trusting our inward journey, we find God at the center, renewing us today and every day with God's healing presence—no matter our circumstances. With God as our center we journey outside our self for energy and fellowship—and inside our self for wisdom and renewal.

When we come to our mats as introverts or extroverts, or maybe a little of both, we accept the invitation to be present. We breathe, settle, and ground ourselves in faith and in the knowledge that we are exactly where we are supposed to be, and we let the inward journey flow. The breath and the *asana* are part of the journey inward toward God. The *savasana* or meditation at the end of class is the final destination, the place where we experience the mystery of God, where we are renewed and made ready to return to life in world.

BREATH PRAYER

Inhale ◆ Day

Exhale ◆ by Day

POSE FOCUS Hero pose, *virasana*, is a wonderful seat from which to begin your inward journey. Often used in meditation, it is a pose that provides an alternative to outward-oriented warrior energy, as the energy of the pose moves inward to produce a peaceful Hero. Despite its promise, Hero pose holds many challenges for our Western bodies and minds. It's a pose in which you essentially sit back on or between your folded legs. Many students find it necessary to prop this pose with bolsters between their thighs and calves or by sitting on a block. A prayer stool may also make the pose more accessible. If you are new to Hero pose, begin with short practices. Gradually increase your time in the pose, as your thighs, hips, and ankles allow. Don't lose heart. Wait for the peaceful renewal promised by drawing inward into this pose.

The Practice of Hearing God Whispers

SCRIPTURE Then he was told, "Go, stand on the mountain at attention before God. God will pass by." A hurricane wind ripped through the mountains and shattered the rocks before God, but God wasn't to be found in the wind; after the wind an earthquake, but God wasn't in the earthquake; and after the earthquake fire, but God wasn't in the fire; and after the fire a gentle and quiet whisper.

1 KINGS 19:11–12 *THE MESSAGE*

SPIRITUAL FOCUS "Let us be silent so we may hear the whisper of God."

RALPH WALDO EMERSON

DEVOTION One of the most sought-after experiences for people of faith is hearing the voice of God. Our own distractibility is one obstacle to our ability to detect God attempting to engage us in conversation. We have become adept multi-taskers, but the most difficult barrier for most of us is our inability to turn down or tune out those incessant, yappy little voices inside our head. While this is not easy, it is true that with practice, in prayer and meditation, we can dial down our busy thoughts and access the sacred silence into which God speaks.

This time of year many people form an intention to increase time spent in contemplative practices, such as prayer and meditation. Prayer is commonly understood to mean speaking to God, while meditation can be understood as listening for God's response. For most people meditation is the more difficult of the two—and the one that requires practice. A favorite yogi once observed that telling people to close down their thoughts is like saying "pink elephant" three times: we become laser-focused on the very thing we want to let go of. When our thoughts spiral, repetition of a sacred word or *mantra* can help bring us back to the moment. Practiced with breath, a repeated sacred word encourages silence and increases our ability to hear God. As Rumi, the great poet-mystic, reminds us, *"There is a voice that doesn't use words, listen."*

Choosing a sacred word may in some sense be considered a work of art. One must "try it on" to see whether it both connects us and opens us to God. There are many possible sacred words from which to choose, but if you don't have one in mind you might try *maranatha*. Derived from Aramaic (the language of Jesus), it translates to "Come, Lord." *Maranatha*, combined with breath, becomes a sacred invitation to be still and listen for the quiet presence of God—for the God whisper.

BREATH PRAYER

Use *Maranatha* or your own sacred word.

Alternatively,

Inhale | Come

Exhale | Lord

POSE FOCUS To prepare for seated meditation, first pick your seat: sit on a chair, kneel in Hero pose or in a pew, or sit on the floor in Easy pose. Come into a posture in which you may remain comfortable and attentive. Set a timer, sit tall, and come into your breath. Repeat to yourself *I am awake, I am alert, I am aware.* On inhalation repeat your sacred word and on exhalation imagine the essence of your word suffusing every cell of your body. Continue repeating your sacred word. When your mind starts to wander pull your attention back with your breath. At some point you may find yourself letting go of the conscious repetition of your sacred word. Listen into this pause. You just might detect a whisper!

The Practice of Walking With

SCRIPTURE He has told you, O mortal, what is good; and what does the Lord require of you but to do justice, and to love kindness, and to walk humbly with your God?

MICAH 6:8

SPIRITUAL FOCUS "We are all just walking each other home."

RAM DASS

DEVOTION Our home state, Minnesota, has a cultural nickname: we are called *Minnesota nice*. A friend from another state pointed out that being "nice," while sometimes helpful, is in other situations not so much . . . Sometimes being helpful actually prevents the person or people in the situation from learning what they need to learn. Sometimes being helpful is operating from our own sense of what is needed in a given situation rather than according to what the other person really needs. Most people who reach out for help are really asking for us to listen, to allow them to process or problem-solve aloud. Most people are looking for our presence rather than our help.

In the ethical yoga practice of *ahimsa*, nonviolence to others, we find an intersection between our ethical practice and our call to be people of faith. What does God require of us? To walk humbly with God and, as a natural byproduct or offshoot of this stance, with our neighbor in need. This can be hard work, since most of us are wired to adopt a "fix-it" mode when presented with a difficulty. If we're honest with ourselves, listening and walking with another, with only our attentive presence to offer—no answers to propose—goes against our grain; still, it's a practice we try to cultivate in yoga, as well as in our faith practice. We can put ourselves at risk for injury by trying to "force" our body into a pose that is unavailable to us. Approaching our yoga practice in the spirit of *ahimsa*, committing ourselves to just listening to our bodies, our minds, and our spirits, is a practice of faith we carry with us from the mat into the world.

BREATH PRAYER

Inhale ◆ I Am

Exhale ◆ Walking

POSE FOCUS Humble or Bound Warrior, *baddha virabhadrasana*, is a lovely pose to add to your Warrior pose repertoire. The movement of the pose is said to simulate bowing down to honor God. Begin in either standing or seated Warrior I, hips facing forward in the pose. Stack your front knee over your ankle and ground your back foot into the mat at a warrior angle. Interlace the hands behind your back and open your heart center. If it is available to you, bend forward with heart leading toward the inside of your front leg. This is a powerful pose that simultaneously stretches and strengthens your body. It is also one that teaches us to lead with the heart, and be humble in the pose.

The Practice of an Open Heart

SCRIPTURE With the eyes of your heart enlightened, you may know what is the hope to which [God] has called you, what are the riches of God's glorious inheritance among the saints.
EPHESIANS 1:18

SPIRITUAL FOCUS "Until we can receive with an open heart, we are never really giving with an open heart."
BRENÉ BROWN

DEVOTION When we love with an open heart—are emotionally available— we trust our feelings enough to share God's love with others. But feelings can be tricky. Sometimes our emotions are glorious and hope-filled and at other times confused or unwelcome. Yogis have a simple practice that helps with feelings—that help us get back to loving with an open heart. It is called a *mudra*. *Mudras* are hand positions that are used to shift our energy or feelings in a more desirable direction, getting us back onto the healing path. Studies have pointed to *mudras* as being beneficial in dealing with chronic pain. Believe it or not, we have all done a *mudra* at one time or another—probably as children, when we have crossed our fingers and hoped for something positive to happen.

A familiar hand position in church that would be considered a *mudra* in the yoga world is our prayer pose. Bringing our hands to our heart in prayer and bowing our head is a posture that we use to open ourselves to be moved in the direction of God's will, of God's desire for us and for all people. Prayer pose shifts our energy to align us more closely with God's Spirit. It opens our hearts to receive the love of God and extend this love to all people.

BREATH PRAYER

Inhale ◆ Open

Exhale ◆ My Heart

POSE FOCUS I often use Fountain Breath to end my classes. It's a flowing *asana* that opens up heart energy and uses prayer hands. Start in Mountain pose or in a comfortable seated position. Bring hands to heart center in Prayer pose and on inhalation raise the hands, palm to palm, above your head, straightening your arms. With an audible exhalation through the mouth, separate the hands and arms out to the sides and then circle them back to your chest, resting your hands once again in Prayer pose. Try syncing three cycles of Fountain Breath with a traditional closing prayer, such as *"In the name of the Creator (Breath), in the name of the Son (Breath), and in the name of the Holy Spirit (Breath), Amen.* Feel the opening of your heart.

The Practice of Open Hands

SCRIPTURE I will bless you as long as I live;
I will lift up my hands and call on your name.

PSALM 63:4

SPIRITUAL FOCUS "I have held many things in my
hands, and I have lost them all; but whatever I have
placed in God's hands, that I still possess."

MARTIN LUTHER

DEVOTION Last week we talked about *mudras*, hand positions that help us reconnect and redirect our energy and emotions in a more positive direction. Used as part of our yoga practice, our hands help us center into our inner sanctuary. More commonly, we use our hands to express our emotions to the world around us. Our hands are one of the body parts we engage when we wish to express the feelings in our heart. Hands raised in praise, a simple peace sign, hands shaped in the form of a heart—all communicate something about us to those around us. When we deliberately practice loving hand gestures, our hands become the hands of God that serve our neighbor.

As we move forward on our spiritual journey and begin to see with our eyes what God sees, and hear with our ears God's voice—as our hearts are opened we witness the very essence of God's love. What does God's love look like? Getting our hands dirty, maybe. Holding a baby— what joy! Holding up a friend or a stranger who is suffering. These are all ways to give away God's love, with our hands and with our hearts. Opening our hands to receive God's love, holding God's love in the sacred space of our hearts, and then handing it over to our neighbor constitutes both a practice and an opportunity that presents itself every day, offering us the opportunity to live our life with intentional integrity and grace.

BREATH PRAYER

Inhale ◆ Lift

Exhale ◆ My Hands

POSE FOCUS This week add *mudras* to all of your seated poses. Two simple *mudras* I use often are hands on my knees, palms either up or down. Use the palms-up hand position to receive needed energy or when you feel yourself to be in particular need of God's love. Use the palms-down hand position when you need grounding—perhaps based on doing too much, thinking too much, . . . or too much of whatever! To determine which *mudra* would be most beneficial in your practice, ask yourself, *What do I need, right now, this moment?* You may find the answer right there in the palms of your hands.

The Practice of Mystery

SCRIPTURE Let me tell you something wonderful,
a mystery I'll probably never fully understand. We're not
all going to die—*but* we are all going to be changed.

1 CORINTHIANS 15:51 *THE MESSAGE*

SPIRITUAL FOCUS "Mystery creates wonder and wonder
is the basis for humankind's desire to understand."

NEIL ARMSTRONG

DEVOTION The mystery of who Jesus is and how he relates to God is one with which first- and twenty-first-century people alike have struggled and with which we continue to grapple. There are so many questions and so many theories about what happened, both on the cross and in the days following. The Jesus narrative is one of death followed by new life—a progression that seems impossible and is hardly verifiable through our logical, cause-and-effect conscious thought patterns. This is a narrative with which we can engage only by allowing ourselves to lean in to the mystery of God.

As faithful people who have studied the stories, we're obliged at the end of the day to conclude that there is much we cannot know or understand. Gaining the confidence to trust in the mystery of God doesn't happen naturally for most of us. Yet we're better able to live in to the story of God when we become comfortable with the unknown and presently unknowable. One place for us to find the trust needed to accommodate mystery, a place to which we can come with all our questions, is on our mats. When we invite God's presence on our mat we create a sanctuary within which we may experience God's assurance. Our mats become a place at which we don't have to "know" anything or everything; a place where paradox can be embraced and pondered. It is natural to desire knowledge, but mystery is a part of our story too. When we embrace the mystery of God, along with the story of God, we find not only knowledge but also faith.

BREATH PRAYER

Inhale ◆ I Embrace

Exhale ◆ the Mystery

POSE FOCUS Reverse Prayer pose, *pashchima namaskarasana*, may seem like a mystery. There are many variations. Take it in gentle steps, always check in with your body and breath and come out of the pose if you experience any joint pain. (1) With breath, raise your hands overhead, with palms together. Bend your elbows, lowering your bent arms to your sides. Enjoy the upper arm stretch. (2) Clasp opposite elbows behind your back, squeeze your shoulder blades together, and breathe through your heart center. (3) Bring palms together behind your back with fingers pointing down. Imagine your collarbone widening with each breath. (4) From variation 3, on an inhalation bring your fingertips in toward your spine as you reverse the hands upward, palms together. No matter the variation, Reverse Prayer pose symbolizes God's grace coming down from above, and that is a mystery worth practicing!

The Practice of a New Day

SCRIPTURE Take action, for it is your duty, and we are with you; be strong, and do it.

EZRA 10:4

SPIRITUAL FOCUS "With a new day comes new strength and new thoughts."

ELEANOR ROOSEVELT

DEVOTION Telling stories is one way to teach and learn new ways of thinking. A local church told the story of Jesus' ministry by blending historical readings of the biblical narrative with music from *Godspell* and *Jesus Christ, Superstar*. At the end of the storytelling the pastor posed the question, *"What difference will this story make for you tomorrow, or the next day?"*

The hoped-for outcome for any storyteller is that the listener might experience the story in a new way, be strengthened in understanding, and proceed to share the story, encouraging others. This new understanding may be subtle or serendipitous: an *Aha!* experience the listener can't wait to share with someone else. Still, when we experience something that feels real and new, it takes courage and strength for us to share that experience with another. It takes courage because sharing exposes our vulnerability: our inspiring new idea might be rejected by others. And yet we are so moved by these stimulating, though unaccustomed thoughts that we can't help but talk about our experience. Sharing takes strength because doing something or talking about our experience makes it real, and living in the real world can be hard work!

When yoga was first becoming popular in the West, people would leave their mats saying, *"I'm not sure what happened here, but I feel great!"* In our faith-based yoga classes we hear a similar comment, *"It's amazing how one can experience the real presence of God when one becomes still."* Sitting with a new thought, idea, or story that speaks truth to our hearts, and then having the courage to share this experience, is one way of living out our life of faith in community. It's a practice that strengthens us to greet each new day with joy.

BREATH PRAYER

Inhale ◆ I Am

Exhale ◆ New

POSE FOCUS Warrior II, *virabhadrasana 2,* is a powerful, weight-bearing pose that is known to strengthen bones. But it is also a source of peaceful warrior energy that brings courage to help us BE in the world. Enter Warrior II with an eye to alignment: knee directed toward the middle toe of the front foot, opening the inner thigh; hips open to the side of your mat, arms stretching long from the shoulders, front and back; jaw relaxed and neck subtle; feet evenly grounded; and core strong. Draw breath into your core center, lighting up your heart center, and on exhalation feel energy emanating out through your limbs, running down each leg to the earth, extending through your arms and hands from front to back fingertips. As you hold the pose, continue using your breath to draw strength into your core center. On exhalation, send out peaceful warrior energy through your limbs . . . and into the world.

The Practice of Healing

SCRIPTURE On either side of the river is the tree of life . . . , and the leaves of the tree are for healing of the nations. Nothing accursed will be found there any more.

REVELATION 22:2–3

SPIRITUAL FOCUS "Health and healing are about more than the eradication of disease. Health is related to wholeness and holy—knowing who we are and how we are connected with the world around us."

DR. LARRY DOSSEY

DEVOTION At a recent healing touch and prayer workshop the healing power of God was shared with a group of participants. At the workshop the attendees learned that the gift of healing is from one source, God. They also learned that each of them has been given gifts of healing to use for themselves and for the healing of others. Most significantly, they learned that all people have within them the healing power of God.

Healing touch, sacred movement, and prayer are ancient faith practices that can be expressed in many ways. As teachers of faith-based yoga, we hope and pray that our breath-centered yoga practice will open our students to the same healing presence of God that we ourselves have experienced. By healing we don't necessarily mean the effecting of a cure. We learn from Jesus' healing ministry that healing and curing aren't the same thing. Healing means being made whole—in body, mind, and spirit. When we practice in the Presence we invite God's healing light to permeate every cell of our bodies, to make us whole. If God can bring healing to the nations via the leaves of a tree . . . think of how delighted God must be to bring healing to us.

Inhale ◆ I Am

Exhale ◆ Connected

POSE FOCUS *Vrkasana*, Tree pose, is a pose my students seem to either love or hate, depending on their sense of balance. But we don't have to put one foot high on our inner thigh and circle both hands overhead in order to experience the full benefits of the pose; a simple "kickstand" foot position on the floor, with one hand on a chair to steady us, will do just as well. The real power in tree pose is not in the physical posture per se but in the integration of our breath and the focus of our busy brains while in the pose. These are key to our achieving balance and wholeness. To find the wholeness in the pose we need to give up judgment and expectations *about* the pose. We need to find, today, the modification that will allow us to experience steadiness and comfort in the pose. We achieve balance in our pose and in our life when we connect body, mind and spirit. Then we can heal.

The Practice of Spiritual Satisfaction

SCRIPTURE If God gives such attention to the appearance of wildflowers—most of which are never even seen—don't you think he'll attend to you, take pride in you, do his best for you? What I'm trying to do here is to get you to relax, to not be so preoccupied with *getting*, so you can respond to God's *giving*. People who don't know God and the way he works fuss over these things, but you know both God and how he works. Steep your life in God-reality, God-initiative, God-provisions. Don't worry about missing out. You'll find all your everyday human concerns will be met.

MATTHEW 6:30–33 *THE MESSAGE*

SPIRITUAL FOCUS "Have patience with all things, but chiefly have patience with yourself."

SAINT FRANCES DE SALES

DEVOTION A yogi and friend of Yogadevotion, Micheal Westbrock, was among the first of our guest teachers to encourage our instructors along the path of spiritual satisfaction. Like most Westerners practicing yoga, we began our journey through the physical practice of the discipline. We were all so anxious to do everything right: correct foot placement, correct head and neck alignment, correct breath pattern. We asked many questions of Micheal and most often got the same response: "*How does it feel?*" Finally, after hearing the same response over and over again, it dawned on us that *doing* everything right wouldn't provide us with the satisfaction we were looking for if we couldn't connect that with how we felt (in other words, with the pose's *feeling* right)! Satisfaction came when we were able to exercise enough patience to just BE in our bodies, to feel and connect with that which was within us.

Micheal affirmed for us that from its inception the practice of yoga was intended as one way to connect with the divine, with the Holy Spirit within us. At the time it was not intuitive for us as Western yoga practitioners to listen to our body and breath in order to connect to the internal teacher, God's Spirit within.

Yoga and faith practices often share an unnecessary felt need to "fuss" over the particulars, when what we really need is the reminder that we already have within us God's promise and presence. We pray that, both in our faith journey and in our yoga practice, we will achieve a greater sense of God and, as in this week's Scripture passage, hear God say "*Relax. I've got this!*"

BREATH PRAYER

Inhale ◆ I Am

Exhale ◆ Satisfied

POSE FOCUS Standing Forward Fold, *uttanasana*, is a lovely pose in which to simply BE. The pose is known to calm the body and mind and is one of those I practice every night before retiring to bed. Come into the pose on an exhalation with knees bent, belly on your thighs. As your hamstrings release, your legs may straighten, but keep your knees soft. Let your eye gaze settle back between your legs so that your head and neck hangs loose. Relax. You've got this! It is especially calming when practiced with a sinking breath of prolonged exhalation. Come into the pose and apply a count to your breath— lengthening the exhalation with each breath cycle. One way to do this is to double your exhalation relative to your inhalation. Start by inhaling to the count of two and exhaling to the count of four. Next, inhale for a count of three and exhale for a count of six. If the ability is available to you, inhale for four counts and exhale for eight. With each exhalation "sink" deeper into the pose, stop fussing, and relax. BE satisfied.

The Practice of Being Made Whole

SCRIPTURE Saving is all [God's] idea, and all his work. All we *do* is trust him enough to let him do it. It's God's gift from start to finish! We don't play the major role. If we did, we'd probably go around bragging that we'd done the whole thing! No, we neither make nor save ourselves. God does both the making and saving.

EPHESIANS 2:8–9 *THE MESSAGE* (emphasis added)

SPIRITUAL FOCUS "Through salvation our past has been forgiven, our present has been given meaning, our future is secured."

RICK WARREN

DEVOTION Have you ever been asked to identify the date on which you "got saved?" This is a standard question in some faith traditions, within which believers understand the word "salvation" as an instantaneous, fixed outcome of the Savior's act of effecting eternal security on our behalf. One second the individual isn't saved, and then—*voile*—they are! However, you might be surprised to learn that the word rendered "salvation" is used almost twice as often in the New Testament to convey a sense of progression, like a verb—the idea of *being saved*. In fact, the term appears 110 times with this sense of movement, to express not a fixed or stagnant moment in time, not a done deal but a process of development—a *being* healed, restored to wholeness, or made whole. The ancient first-century Israelites of Jesus' day were far less concerned about being saved in eternity and far more concerned with being made whole or healed in the present, in the here and now (in their case, I suppose, in the there and then). Healing and wholeness constituted a primary mission and message for Jesus, and through the inner working of the Holy Spirit these incomparable healing benefits continue to be available to us.

One of the most powerful teachings in yoga is how to be present (adjective) in the present (noun)—to be focused on and engaged with the here and now. When we practice *pranayama* (breath) or *asana* (physical movement), our attention is drawn to the present moment, the now, bringing focus and awareness to our minds. We experience harmony as our body, mind, and spirit work together in sync. But the breath, movement, and mind focus, while healing for our bodies and minds, are only part of the reality. We are made whole by God's grace, which we experience in the relationship with God for which we were created. Trusting God to make us whole is a faith discipline we can practice both on our mats and in our lives out in the world.

BREATH PRAYER

Inhale ◆ I Am

Exhale ◆ Whole

POSE FOCUS Sometimes we need a challenging pose to bring our body, breath, and mind into the present. Plank pose, *phalakasana*, and its variations can be especially demanding, but many students find the challenge worth the effort, as benefits of the pose include increased core strength and improved posture. Whether you practice plank with knees on or off the mat or at a wall, be sure to engage your abdominal muscles in the pose to protect your lower back. While holding the pose, bring your attention to your breath, keeping it steady and deep—this may be your greatest challenge in the pose! Be fully present. Be whole.

The Practice of Blessedness

SCRIPTURE "Blessed are the pure in heart, for they will see God."
MATTHEW 5:8

SPIRITUAL FOCUS "Blessed is the influence of
one true, loving human soul on another."
GEORGE ELIOT

DEVOTION Purity is the topic of many sacred Scripture passages. Do's and don'ts prescribe for adherents the rules for living a moral, ethical life. Famously, Jesus reformulated the ancient laws, summarizing the Ten Commandments as loving God and loving our neighbor as much as we love ourselves. Yoga has ethical observances called *niyamas*. The first, *saucha*, is that of purity—of *cleaning up our act*, so to speak. One way to do this that directly benefits both our neighbor and our self is to pause to examine our thoughts before we voice them. Think about that aggravating person in your acquaintance who can always be counted on to say no before you've finished expressing your question. Or about a time when you misspoke—or spoke too fast—and inadvertently offended someone.

Our thoughts often evolve in three stages: initially, a thought is unformed or only poorly formulated, containing an element of emotion that may be inappropriate, unnecessary, or unhelpful to express; we call this a knee-jerk reaction. The second iteration of a thought (there's a reason we call it a "second thought") may be better formed but is often still not in a format the other person will hear, understand, or accept. The third and final phase of the thought process, in terms of its verbal expression, tends to be more refined and better articulated; if we can wait for it, we'll use more carefully chosen words that the listener will hear and accept.

Learning to think before we speak—better still, to invite God to inform our thoughts before we engage our tongues—can be difficult but immensely rewarding, as the result is often improved relations with our neighbor. Similarly, cleaning up our act in our yoga practice begins when we start noticing, without judgment, where our thoughts wander while we're in a pose. By acknowledging our thought drift we can learn to let go of distracting thoughts and to gently return our attention to our present reality. We can discern without haste what no longer serves us and intentionally let it go. Examining our thoughts before we speak or act is a practice that blesses both us and others.

BREATH PRAYER

Inhale ◆ I Am

Exhale ◆ Blessed

POSE FOCUS Heart-opening poses symbolically represent a pure spirit: heart first and foremost, body and head following. This week add an extra heart opening pose into your practice—one in which you squeeze your shoulder blades together to open your heart center. Bow pose, *dhanurasana*, is a powerful heart opener. Lie on your belly, bend your legs, hold your ankles, or circle your ankles with a strap. Press your ankles into your hands or strap as you lift your legs off the mat, simultaneously lifting your chest and head as well. Your abdominal muscles will have less room to move, so remember to breathe into your back body. Let your heart energy shine forth, front and center.

The Practice of Liberation

SCRIPTURE [The woman] was bent over and was quite unable to stand up straight. When Jesus saw her, he called her over and said, "Woman, you are set free from your ailment." When he laid his hands on her, immediately she stood up straight and began praising God.

LUKE 13:11–13

SPIRITUAL FOCUS "For to be free is not merely to cast off one's chains, but to live in a way that respects and enhances the freedom of others."

NELSON MANDELA

DEVOTION It has been said that Jesus' ministry on earth was comprised of one-third preaching, one-third teaching, and one-third healing. The story in our passage today relates one of the many miraculous healings Jesus performed. The woman, crippled and bent over for 18 years, is healed by Jesus' words and touch. Jesus, who had been teaching in the synagogue, caught sight of her, stopped teaching, called her over, and healed her, setting her free. The woman was a daughter of Abraham (a Jewess) who was present in the synagogue because she was a woman of faith. One encounter with Jesus and she found herself liberated from pain and suffering; she had been made whole. Jesus' healing the hunched-over woman, though, is only part of the story. He performed this miracle on the Sabbath, and healing on the Sabbath was considered work and was therefore forbidden. Jesus, knowing this prohibition full well, healed her anyway. The priests and scribes were furious, having more concern for the law than for the fact that Jesus had just liberated this woman from nearly two decades of relentless pain and suffering.

In her sermon on this moving story Rev. Barbara Lundblad notes the reaction of the religious leaders: "*How can it be that the liberation of one threatens another? Isn't liberation of one liberation for all?*"

We bring integrity to our yoga practice when we honor our body. We are free (and encouraged) to modify our poses as needed, and that freedom liberates us to experience the practice more fully. Interestingly, when we choose to modify a pose in class, we not only experience the benefits ourselves but give visual permission to our neighbor to exercise the freedom to modify as well. A liberated yoga practice—like a liberated faith practice—embraces freedom, threatens no one, and carries the potential of freedom for all.

BREATH PRAYER

Inhale ◆ I Am

Exhale ◆ Free

POSE FOCUS Dancer, *natara-jasana*, is a beautiful pose with many variations. One popular modification is to bring the free hand to a wall for support. In my chair yoga class I have students put their free hand on a secure chair back and use a strap in the other hand to bend one leg. When modifying a pose it is important to remember and honor its essence. Dancer is a balance pose, but it is also a heart-opener. The chest is lifted and open, while the lower back is relaxed and long. Flex the lifted foot to help keep the knee aligned. Always use your breath to determine the most beneficial modification for your body. It is only when the breath is deep and calm and the body is comfortable and steady that you will find free-dom in the pose.

The Practice of Hitting the Pause Button

SCRIPTURE God is our refuge and strength, a very present help in trouble. Therefore we will not fear, though the earth should change, though the mountains shake in the heart of the sea; though its waters roar and foam, though the mountains tremble with its tumult. Selah.

PSALM 46:1-3

SPIRITUAL FOCUS "Silence is the pause in me when I am near to God."

ARVO PART

DEVOTION Imagine an ordinary day. The stars seem to be aligned, everybody around you is functioning as expected, and every plan is unfolding just as you had hoped. And then the world turns. Not a life-or-death crisis, perhaps, but one niggling distraction after another that causes you to wonder what's going on. Our human instinct in response to each disruption is to react quickly, make an immediate decision, and try to return to our previous state of homeostasis or balance. While that may be our go-to mode of operation, the practice of pausing may be more helpful.

Throughout the psalms we repeatedly encounter challenging situations people faced. They were reminded over and over again in the Hebrew scriptures that God was their refuge and shield. Many such proclamations in the psalms are followed by the Hebrew word *selah*. Some suggest that the term indicated a pause—like a rest in a musical score—possibly in a narrative story set to music. Others believe the expression signified a designated place in the poetry for one to pause, reflect, and consider God's promised presence before acting.

Pausing to reflect is difficult for a generation programmed toward DOing. We tend to value decisive action, speedy problem solving, and conclusive follow-through. Interestingly, when we do find ourselves able to pause, reflect, and trust God's promised presence, we may see paths through our dilemmas that might not otherwise have occurred to us. Hitting the pause button is a discipline that involves stopping, connecting with our breath, being intentionally silent in the moment, and recognizing that our *now* doesn't have to equate to our *forever*. The breath calms our reactive system and gives focus to our overactive, solution-oriented minds. Taking a break, pausing to reflect and remember God's promised protection is a faith practice that serves us daily, as we live off our mats and into the world.

BREATH PRAYER

Inhale ◆ Se

Exhale ◆ la-a-ah

POSE FOCUS Pausing to take a breath in the midst of life's challenges can be difficult. Hand to Foot pose, *utthita hasta padangusthasana,* is one I find so challenging I have to push myself to practice it. There's a lot going on in this pose: balance, muscle stretching, hip opening, and coordination. Take it in small, preparatory steps. Using a strap, start in a supine version of the pose, practicing this version until you're comfortable in the pose on your back. Now approach the standing pose, perhaps using a chair placed by a wall as a prop. Place your raised leg on the chair pushing into the wall with your heel. Over time, as your body allows, graduate to a higher leg position by placing blankets on the chair. At some point, when your body is ready, use a strap to lift your leg off the chair. Regardless of what expression of the pose is currently available to you, pause and rest in the pose. *Selah!*

The Practice of One Language

SCRIPTURE When the day of Pentecost had come, they were all together in one place. And suddenly from heaven there came a sound like the rush of a violent wind, and it filled the entire house where they were sitting. Divided tongues, as of fire, appeared among them, and a tongue rested on each of them. All of them were filled with the Holy Spirit and began to speak in other languages, as the Spirit gave them ability.

ACTS 2:1–4

SPIRITUAL FOCUS "Your spirit is mingled with mine . . . what touches you, touches me."

RUMI

DEVOTION Pentecost, one of the most energy-filled festivals of the church, celebrates the reality that we can all be different, speak different languages, and still understand each other. We are all loved by God, and each of us can love God and others in our own way. The festival is filled with images of fire and flame, wind and breath. These two sets of elements are directly connected, so that one cannot survive without the other. Without air a flame is suffocated, and without the fire of purpose human breath becomes cold and lifeless. Mingled together, both thrive.

The images in this passage inspire us to consider that while we human beings may speak different languages we are all infused with one Spirit and are loved by one God. God comes to us in many different ways to remind us that we together constitute *one* people. When celebrated, our shared humanity allows us not just to live together but to thrive together.

In the early years of yoga's resurgence in America, many teachers preferred English names for the *asanas* over their traditional Sanskrit names. One reason for this preference was to help students readily understand each practice. But the other—and perhaps the primary—motivation to use English translations of the pose names was fear. Fear of misunderstanding distracted people from the benefits of the yoga practice. Sanskrit is, however, a beautiful language, and lovely sounding words like *savasana* and *namaste* are now better understood to mean rest and a greeting of honor, respectively. They reflect yoga concepts that are of mutual benefit for all participants who wish to live in collective harmony. Much as our faith teaches us to trust the Spirit, we as yogis trust the Spirit to enter into our faith and yoga practices to lead the way so we can live peacefully and thrive in union with the One who loves us and each other.

BREATH PRAYER

Inhale ◆ We

Exhale ◆ Are One

POSE FOCUS When I first heard the English translation of *gomukhasana*, Cow Face pose, I laughed aloud. Yet I was perplexed, wondering what that unlikely sounding name could possibly imply for the pose. Over the years, though, I've come to apply a kind of bovine docility to my practice of this pose, not pushing myself to exceed my bodily limitations in the *asana*. Cow Face pose is known as both a hip- and upper back-opener; shoulders and knees need to be amenable to the pose as well. This week, add a version of Cow Face pose to your practice and discover for yourself how it translates.

The Practice of Managing Fear

SCRIPTURE God is love. When we take up permanent residence in the life of love, we live in God and God lives in us. This way, love has the run of the house, becomes at home and mature in us, so that we're free of worry on Judgment Day—our standing in the world is identical with Christ's. There is no room in love for fear. Well-formed love banishes fear.

1 JOHN 4:18 *THE MESSAGE*

SPIRITUAL FOCUS "Not being in control brings fear. Remembering God's in control brings peace."

UNKNOWN AUTHOR

DEVOTION A recent posting on Facebook drew a great deal of attention. The quote read, "*Sometimes the fear won't go away, so you just have to do it afraid.*" The large number of people who responded to this statement constituted a not so subtle reminder that fear is something we have all experienced and, to a greater or lesser degree, tried to manage. Fear can be a protective mechanism in our fight-or-flight response to danger. But fear can also keep us locked in a "known"—as in status quo—situation that, even if it's less than exciting or challenging, makes us feel complacent and safe. The process of identifying, confronting, and exploring our fears is a spiritual practice that might be the next beneficial step in our faith journey.

While it's true that we may have to confront a situation even if we're feeling anxious or frightened about it, Scripture promises that we'll never be alone in this venture. God's presence, which is ever with us, has the power to cast out our fears. Connecting with the Holy Spirit to experience the love that banishes all fear puts us in tune with our "God inklings"—with that "Holy itch," some call a "God smack" that reminds us of the holy paradox that we live in God and God lives in us. Given that degree of inter-connectedness, how could we possibly have anything to fear?

For some of us stepping onto our yoga mat for the first time produced fear, while for others getting quiet enough to come to a place of disclosure, and therefore of vulnerability, holds an element of anxiety. In that still place we just might find ourselves forced to confront uncomfortable truths that threaten to distance us from our relationship with God, issues we would much rather ignore. But as we practice remembering that God's love is greater than all of our fears, as we find in our faith the confidence that love overcomes fear, our apprehensions will be banished, leaving peace in their wake.

BREATH PRAYER

Inhale ◆ All Love

Exhale ◆ No Fear

POSE FOCUS Chest-opening poses strengthen our heart-center energy, supporting us to live in love. Add an extra heart-opening pose into this week's practice. Camel pose, *ustrasana*, is a powerful heart-opener. Since it is important while in the pose not to compress the back of the neck or the lower back, begin your practice with modifications and props. Start in a kneeling position. Bring your hands to the small of your back, palms flat and fingers pointing down, chest open. Lengthen from your tailbone to the crown of your head. Breathe. You can also use a chair as a prop. Kneel before a chair so that your back side touches the edge of the seat. With breath reach around and hold the sides of the chair. Lengthen your spine, open your chest, and breathe into your heart center: *All Love*.

The Practice of Slowing Down

SCRIPTURE True to your word, you let me catch my breath and send me in the right direction.

PSALM 23:3 *THE MESSAGE*

SPIRITUAL FOCUS "Slow down and everything you are chasing will come around and catch you."

JOHN DEPAOLA

DEVOTION Randomly, spontaneously, a young man decided to take a walk through the park. Simply ambling along the pathway, enjoying the birdsong, appreciating the variety of plant life; and drawing slow, deep breaths was refreshing. Pausing for a short time to catch his breath and formulate his thoughts, he was rewarded with an immediate sense of calm. But not much farther into the walk people started whizzing past him on their bikes with cautioning cries of "*On your left!*" Speed walkers strode past him, almost elbowing him off the path. When he came across some friends, they ran in place while talking with him, not wanting to disrupt their workout. And when he inquired, "*How are you?*" they responded with audible sighs, "*BUSY!*"

We all recognize ourselves in this scene, either as the one stopping to catch our breath or as the one who is trying to squeeze in a walk in the form of a workout. Omid Safi, a writer for the radio show *On Being* and a professor at Duke University, expresses it this way: "*This disease of being 'busy' (and let's call it what it is, the dis-ease of being busy, when we are never at ease) is spiritually destructive to our health and wellbeing. It saps our ability to be fully present with those we love the most, our families, and keeps us from forming the kind of community that we all so desperately crave.*"

Our Scripture verse for today is from a familiar passage that promises that we *can* rest and catch our breath and that God will not only guard our time but will help us get back on to the path of healing and wholeness. Our yoga practice teaches us how to catch our breath through *asana*, meditation, and simply practicing. The invitation to slow down and just breathe is found at the crossroads of yoga and faith practices. Pausing to regain our perspective reinforces the promise that God longs to—and can—cure our dis-ease of busyness.

BREATH PRAYER

Inhale ◆ I Will

Exhale ◆ Slow Down

POSE FOCUS I remember being told when I first started practicing yoga that Downward Facing Dog, *adho mukha svanasana*, was considered a resting pose. "*You've got to be kidding*," I thought to myself, all too aware of my aching calves and arms. It's funny how things change. Today I love to come into Down Dog during a *vinyasa* flow to rest and come back to my breath. Modifying the pose may be the key for many to find the promised rest in the pose. Placing hands on blocks, a chair, or a wall can create variation and comfort in the pose. Knees may be bent or remain on the floor. All we really need to do in Down Dog is slow down: to come into our breath, lengthen the torso as we open our heart center, and rest.

The Practice of Three Things

SCRIPTURE Though one might prevail against another, two will withstand one. A threefold cord is not quickly broken.
ECCLESIASTES 4:12

SPIRITUAL FOCUS "In three words I can sum up everything I have learned about life: it goes on."
ROBERT FROST

DEVOTION Have you heard the saying *"Things happen in threes"*? When we practice *asana*, we speak of entering a pose, modifying the pose, and then resting in the pose. And when therapists offer healing massage they speak of three touches: the first is new, the second familiar, and the third relaxing. Recently, a Yogadevotion instructor related to our teacher group something she had learned at a yoga conference. She taught us about the three student *doshas*, personality archetypes that are described in traditional *Ayurvedic* healing practices, and about how to sequence a yoga flow to accommodate all three types of student: complacent, distracted, or striving. Working within the pattern of three feels natural and comprehensive.

In the Bible the number three is important too, with associations of solid, real, and complete. A basic tenet of the Christian faith is belief in the Trinity—in God the Creator, God the Son, and God the Holy Spirit—and the apostle Paul speaks of the triad of hope, faith, and love. In both instances three represents a complete, integrated relationship.

This week's verse is often quoted at weddings, emphasizing the fact that two are better and stronger than one and that three are complete, especially if the third member of the alliance, God, is included. If there is one common criticism of yoga and faith practices, it is that they are too often all about ourselves. The relationship we experience with God challenges that focus. What we learn on our mat about ourselves and our relationship with God has significant ramifications for the world beyond the mat. A faith-based yoga practice that understands the unique relationship among the three pillars—God, self, and the world—is complete.

BREATH PRAYER

Inhale ◆ I Am

Exhale ◆ Complete

POSE FOCUS Triangle, *trikonasana*, is a favorite pose of many yoga students. For years when I attended class I heard Triangle cued using these words: "*Imagine your body sandwiched between two horizontal planes of glass.*" Ouch! While it is true that we set up the pose as a side stretch, it is important that in so doing we ensure that our knees are not strained. To help the knees find their proper position in the pose we may need to widen or shorten our stance. Protect your knees further by lifting the arches of your feet and your kneecaps as you press the four corners of your feet into the earth. With breath draw energy up both legs to your core center. Keep arms and legs active as you complete the triangle.

The Practice of Breathing through the Storms

SCRIPTURE For God has not given us a spirit of fear, but of power and of love and of a sound mind.
2 TIMOTHY 1:7 *NKJV*

SPIRITUAL FOCUS "Slow breathing is like an anchor in the midst of an emotional storm: the anchor won't make the storm go away but it will hold you steady until it passes."
RUSS HARRIS

DEVOTION Thunderstorms are often one of the first childhood experiences that instill fear. Even for us as adults, when a storm hits we don't always know whether it's going to be a threatening experience or an exhilarating sound and light show. If our very first experience of a storm, though, was an exciting display of nature's wonder (whether or not we consciously recall the event), we may for the rest of our lives find ourselves suffused with a sense of joyful anticipation as we observe a darkening skyscape. If our first experience was scary, on the other hand—perhaps involving a loss of power and the need to stumble to shelter in the dark, possibly disconnected from those we loved—we may for the rest of our lives find the experience or riding out a storm disconcerting; we'll have to work hard to anchor ourselves when the next storm comes, as it inevitably will.

Storms are an ideal metaphor for the challenging circumstances we all face in life. Our past experience informs our present reaction, so when our present challenges evoke past fears we may experience a kind of brain freeze. This is a natural response to fear, but it isn't the only possible response. We have another option, an anchor for all situations; it's something so simple, accessible, and necessary we can do it on a deliberate, conscious level—b-r-e-a-t-h-e. Whether we experience storms on a small or grand scale, breathing through them steadies us, allowing us to think and act appropriately in the moment of crisis.

Scripture reminds us over and over again to "*fear not.*" In our yoga practice we are encouraged to breathe, to resist holding our breath as we hold a pose, and to check in to our breath to determine whether it's safe for us to remain in a pose. Slow and steady breathing not only aids our yoga practice but also helps us weather the vicissitudes of life, allowing our minds to think clearly and our bodies to respond appropriately. Our ever-present breath is a reminder that God has promised to be with us. Learning to breathe *through* the challenging, as well as the beautiful, storms in our lives is a practice that anchors us to trust in God's promised Presence.

BREATH PRAYER

Inhale ◆ I Will

Exhale ◆ Breathe

POSE FOCUS In the mid 1970s a renowned Harvard Medical Center researcher, Dr. Herbert Benson, wrote a book titled *The Relaxation Response*, in which he documented a technique to lower blood pressure and decrease the production of cortisol, a hormone that is released when the body or mind is stressed. It's a technique that yogis have practiced for centuries: slow exhalation. Easily portable, this can be done anywhere: whether sitting in a traffic jam or waiting in a dentist's reception room. This week, whenever you find a storm brewing, practice slowing your exhalation *off* your mat. Sighing is a great way to get started. When we sigh we inhale deeply and prolong our exhalation with a sounding breath; this happens organically. It's a form of wisdom our body instinctively knows.

The Practice of A Third Way

SCRIPTURE "You have heard that it was said, 'You shall love your neighbor and hate your enemy.' But I say to you, Love your enemies and pray for those who persecute you."

MATTHEW 5:43–44

SPIRITUAL FOCUS "Do I not destroy my enemies when I make them my friends?"

ABRAHAM LINCOLN

DEVOTION One reason the teachings of Jesus today referred to as the Sermon on the Mount were so radical is that the lessons were opposite to those taught by the religious leaders of the day, who promoted a "we versus they" interpretation of the law. To some in the crowd who heard the Sermon on the Mount, it might have seemed as though Jesus had come to abolish the law. This was unacceptable to many, but to those who were excluded from Jewish society, based on the standard interpretation of the law, Jesus' words brought new hope. In truth, the teachings of the Sermon on the Mount neither affirmed nor denied the law. Jesus was teaching a third way.

Jesus' point was that the law in and of itself was good—a gift from God intended to promote mutual and reciprocal love, one for another. Jesus taught that we experience God's love through loving and praying for those with whom we are at odds. The highest intention of the law was to be in loving relationship with God and with each other.

In our faith-based yoga practice we are invited to explore Jesus' third way. When a yoga instructor offers cues to guide a student into an *asana*, the student must test those cues, grasp the instructor's description of the *asana's* intention, and be directed into the pose by listening to their own body, heeding the voice of the teacher within. To incorporate Jesus' third way into our yoga practice we need to first find the essence of the *asana*. This gives us the freedom to adapt the pose, still feeling its full benefit even as we reflect the individual needs we sense in our bodies, minds, and spirits. What we learn from practicing the third way on our mats informs us how we are to live as people of faith. When the intentions of our thoughts and actions point to a loving relationship with our neighbor, we are following the third way.

BREATH PRAYER

Inhale ◆ I Am

Exhale ◆ Following

POSE FOCUS Adaptive yoga, is a powerful practice. Originally designed to make yoga accessible to persons with disabilities, it has evolved into a practice for everyBODY that teaches students to find and practice the essence of each pose, and express that essence according to their abilities. To practice an adaptive yoga pose, consider a pose that currently is beyond your physical capabilities— maybe that pose is Side Plank, *vasisthasana*. The pose is both an arm balance and a core strengthener. Ask yourself, *what is this pose DOing?* And equally important, *what is this pose NOT doing?* Let your answer be respectful of the traditional pose, but don't get caught up in any "shoulds." Instead, honor the essence of the pose in your practice, and adapt accordingly. Perhaps your adaptation might include leaning into a wall from a standing position, braced by your hand and arm. Perhaps your adaptation might evolve from a seated position, belly contracted, and back long. Adapt and find a third way to practice.

The Practice of Sustainability

SCRIPTURE But surely, God is my helper;
The Lord is the upholder of my life.

PSALM 54:4

SPIRITUAL FOCUS "Change leads to disappointment
if it is not sustained. Transformation is sustained
change, and it is achieved through practice."

B. K. S. IYENGAR

DEVOTION The word *sustainability* has in recent times been tied to conversations about the environment, but the concept of sustainability informs our lives in many other ways too. Once a good idea has come to fruition or an eye-opening experience changes our perspective, the real work begins: that of sustaining that idea or change.

To sustain something is to develop strategies to ensure that it will endure, to plan for the long term success of that which we wish to maintain. A sustained faith is a faith that endures through joy and sorrow, always trusting God's Spirit to support us, and a sustained yoga lifestyle is one that doesn't fluctuate with the latest trends or most popular classes but is informed by the historic yoga philosophies of peace, no harm, discipline, and contentment. A sustained faith life and enduring yoga lifestyle can both be transformative, but each takes practice. What this practice looks like may be different for each of us, but we need to choose those practices that are life affirming rather than life draining. In order for them to be transformative the practices we choose need to benefit not only our personal lives but our relationship with God and with each other.

The simple beauty of a sustained faith is that we need only trust God, who promises to nourish and sustain our faith. When we practice trusting God the discipline transforms our life. The simple beauty of an enduring yoga practice is that it creates space for us to connect with God. Practice and be transformed.

BREATH PRAYER

Inhale ◆ I Am

Exhale ◆ Transformed

POSE FOCUS Extended Side Angle, *utthita parsvakonasana*, is one of my favorite poses to practice in the morning: the side stretch feels so good! There are many ways to modify the pose to support the torso: front arm or hand on a chair, on your thigh, on a block, or on the floor. When I learned to anchor my back foot into the earth and draw up energy from the ground through my side body and out through my fingertips, I thought *"Wow! I've got this pose."* Recently however, I have come to discover the heart-opening aspect of the pose as well; I now check my alignment to make sure my front body is lifted and open while I keep my neck in a comfortable position, not straining. Opening my heart-center in Extended Side Angle transformed the pose for me. Keeping your heart open through changing situations is transformative off the mat as well.

The Practice of Being a Blessing

SCRIPTURE Do not neglect to do good and to share what you have, for such sacrifices are pleasing to God.
HEBREWS 13:16

SPIRITUAL FOCUS "We make a living by what we get. We make a life by what we give."
WINSTON CHURCHILL

DEVOTION A national news program did a piece on something called the "Happiness Project." The book by the same title, which started out as one woman's quest to find habits that would increase her happiness, became a blockbuster bestseller and spawned a national movement of small groups that meet regularly to discuss their happiness habits. The book described habits that are consistently reported by folks in the pursuit of happiness. One of these is making a list each morning of three things for which they are grateful, and another is meditating and/or praying for 20 minutes each day. Finally, respondents reported doing at least one random act of kindness each day. These are the "musts" they have found are needed to be happy.

In Jesus' teachings found in Matthew 5:1–11, a portion of his Sermon on the Mount referred to today as the Beatitudes, the word rendered "blessed" in many Bible versions is sometimes translated "happy." As we see in many Old Testament stories, the conferring or receiving of a verbal blessing was a highly valued Jewish cultural and religious practice. People celebrated with joy when they had been blessed; happy, many no doubt went on to share that happiness with others. The practice of meditating upon how God has blessed us and then passing forward our gift in order to bless another is a practice that not only brings us happiness but forms us into the kind of community of love that is pleasing to God.

BREATH PRAYER

Inhale ◆ Be

Exhale ◆ a Blessing

POSE FOCUS In the ancient yoga teachings *karma* yoga describes acts of kindness—the practice of selfless action. Regardless of what you call it, this week add into each day at least two acts of kindness to another: one toward a person you know and the other toward a stranger. In both cases perform the kindness without thought to being thanked or even noticed. Perhaps you might offer the last available shopping cart to the person behind you at the grocery store. Or you might wait for another car to pull up to the only open gasoline pump at the station. Maybe you pick up your neighbor's newspaper that has fallen into the street and place it on his or her front porch. Being a blessing is a powerful practice that both enriches the world and nourishes our own souls.

The Practice of Saying I Don't Know

SCRIPTURE This extraordinary plan of God is becoming known and talked about even among the angels!
EPHESIANS 3:10 *THE MESSAGE*

SPIRITUAL FOCUS "Whoever undertakes to set himself up as the judge of truth and knowledge is shipwrecked by the laughter of the gods."
ALBERT EINSTEIN

DEVOTION A mentor and friend of Yogadevotion operated under an interesting motto: "*You don't know what you don't know.*" In a world that pursues and values knowledge one of the hardest statements to make is "*I don't know.*" Our reason-oriented Western minds are challenged by the unknown, and our response to such a challenge is often to gather more information, to search for answers. In the medical and scientific world there is a continuous sense of "becoming," an impetus toward the ongoing gathering of facts that may lead to new discoveries and, ultimately, in some cases, to lives saved; in reality, though, this proliferation of knowledge often leads to more unanswered questions.

The same is true in our faith journey. It is quite true that, as we become more knowledgeable about God, God reveals to us much that is life-giving. And yet there remains a "becoming," an aura of mystery about God that continues to elude our grasp. We must resist the urge to claim certain, fixed knowledge when it comes to God. It takes wisdom to discern what is knowable and what—at least for the present—remains off limits to us. It takes faith to be satisfied with limited, unfolding disclosure.

In our faith and yoga practice we rely on God to continually be present and at the same time we admit that we will never in this life understand God fully. We embrace both the known and the unknown, the certain and the elusive. We can say "*I don't know, but by faith I believe,*" all the while cherishing the mystery. In yoga too, many have practiced and experienced an unexplained, profound sense of peace and renewal. A wise teacher will not try to explain what has happened but will leave the student to wonder about a mysterious experience. We may know much about the biology, psychology, and theology of life, but there is far more that we don't know—and to pretend we do certainly makes God laugh!

BREATH PRAYER

Inhale ◆ By faith

Exhale ◆ I Believe

POSE FOCUS Have you ever been in a yoga class and watched a particularly limber student move into a physically difficult pose? Perhaps you said to yourself in a tone of envy or admiration, "*I don't know how s/he does it.*" Many inverted yoga poses, such as Plough, *halasana*, can be daunting and should be attempted only under the supervision of an experienced yoga teacher. But remember that, at its center, Plough is just another inversion, and give yourself permission to modify the pose or choose another inversion that is safer for your body, such as Legs Up the Wall or, perhaps, Bridge. The *advanced* yoga student is not the strongest or most limber student in the class but the student who, with breath, seeks steadiness and ease in each pose, modifying as needed and inviting God's Presence. And that's no mystery.

The Practice of Community Life

SCRIPTURE Let us consider how we may spur one another on toward love and good deeds, not giving up meeting together, as some are in the habit of doing, but encouraging one another—and all the more as you see the Day approaching.

HEBREWS 10:24–25 *NIV*

SPIRITUAL FOCUS "God came to my house and asked for charity. And I fell on my knees and cried, 'Beloved, what may I give?' 'Just love', He said. 'Just love.'"

SAINT FRANCIS OF ASSISI,
translated by DANIEL LADINSKY

DEVOTION *Communicatio Santorum* is a beautiful Latin phrase that means "community of saints." Many of us think of God as singular, but from the very beginning of Scripture God speaks of community within creation—within what we refer to as the godhead. In Genesis 1:26 God says, "Let *us* make humankind in *our* image." The triune God and heavenly hosts value and create community.

We were fashioned in God's image, and that involves being in relationship with God and with each other because none of us can get through life on our own. When relationships break down we falter, and our faith reminds us to step back from actions that remove us from being in loving community.

In yoga we are encouraged to BE, and that includes being still. Many Christians are uncomfortable with stillness, believing on the basis of James 2:14–19 that faith not backed up by continuous, and even frenetic, activity is a dead faith. James's point is valid and important, of course, but the healthy Godly life entails a "both/and" balance when it comes to contemplation and action, stillness and movement. We practice being present to God while savoring that relationship. And we learn from the life of Jesus how to live in community, how to move from stillness to action, all the while loving our neighbor. In this way we encourage each other both to BE and to DO good deeds motivated by love.

BREATH PRAYER

Inhale ◆ Just

Exhale ◆ Love

POSE FOCUS This week bring balance to your life by practicing yoga both on and off your mat. On your mat find a time each day to BE present to God in stillness. Set a timer and commit yourself to this discipline each day. Off the mat find a time and place to DO in loving community. Perhaps you find this community in your family, your neighborhood, or your church. The practice—the part that takes work—is to be *fully* present while you Be or Do. Listen actively, participating without expectations or judgments; but most important, just love.

The Practice of Imperfection

SCRIPTURE Whoever keeps God's word, in [them] truly the love of God is perfected. By this we may know that we are in God.

1 JOHN 2:5 *ESV*

SPIRITUAL FOCUS "The secret to loving others despite their imperfections is loving ourselves despite ours."

L. R. K. NOST

DEVOTION Witnessing the imperfect nature of our world, our nation, and our communities, one might conclude that we have no need to *practice* imperfection; we're already quite perfect at being imperfect. The practice of embracing our imperfection, however, has to do with identifying that which is imperfect in ourselves and owning it in such a way that it teaches us to acknowledge our shared humanity with those we may dislike or with whom we may disagree.

In the early years of yoga in the West, most teacher trainings revolved around cues intended to help the student achieve the perfect pose. A cue that freed many students and instructors from this notion, liberating them to experience the true benefits of yoga, was attributed to Baron Baptiste when he pointed out, "*There is no perfect pose.*" There is indeed no perfect pose . . . except the one that is right for *you* in your body.

In faith we are called to be one people, united in God's love. Truth be told, God loves us just as we are: as an imperfect and broken humanity. God does not leave us in our brokenness, however; God is always about the business of restoring and reclaiming us back into loving relationship with Godself and with each other. We participate in the relationship by loving ourselves—imperfections and all—and loving our neighbors just as they are. Practice owning your yoga practice right where you are; rest in the perfect knowledge of God's love, and watch the world change!

Inhale ◆ Loved

Exhale ◆ as I Am

POSE FOCUS Boat, *navasana,* is a pose that I longed for years to perfect. With arms and legs both long and lifted, the pose when traditionally executed makes it look as though you are ready to levitate off the ground! As time passed I viewed with increasing dissatisfaction my inability to straighten my legs in the pose. I found myself so frustrated, in fact, that for a time I even stopped practicing it. And then something happened. I let go of my expectations and personal judgments about how I *should* be doing the pose and instead embraced how I *was* doing it. And do you know what? Doing Boat pose with my legs bent turned out to be just fine. After all these years of striving to perfect it I finally *found* the pose, *my* Boat. This week, practice a pose that has been frustrating you. Let go of expectations and judgment and find the pose, just as you are.

The Practice of Holy Breathing

SCRIPTURE How can I, your servant, talk with you, my lord? My strength is gone and I can hardly breathe.
DANIEL 10:17 *NIV*

SPIRITUAL FOCUS "The earth inhales God, why should we not do the same?"
SAINT THOMAS AQUINAS

DEVOTION As I was growing up, when I was upset my mother would counsel me to "*take a deep breath and count to three.*" Invariably I would become calmer, if only temporarily, but enough so that I could tell her what was troubling me. In pausing to find my breath I could move beyond the feelings that were overwhelming me, back into the moment and into the relationship in which I could talk out my problems and respond to my mother's soothing words.

Finding our breath can be difficult, especially when we're caught up in strong emotions, but Scripture teaches us that in doing so we're enabled to "hear" the voice of God. The Hebrew word *ruach* can be translated either as "breath" or "spirit" and appears throughout the Hebrew Scriptures nearly 400 times. In Genesis, where God's life-giving breath is pictured as *ruach*, life is said to be "breathed" into clay. Similarly in the New Testament, the Greek *pneuma* can be translated either as "breath" or as "spirit." In the book of Acts the presence of the Holy Spirit appears as *pneuma*. There is wisdom in these historic words, whose double meanings direct us to find God through our breath.

Like the ancient Jews and Christians, yogis have long understood the connection between breath and spirit. The yoga practice of *pranayama* is often viewed as breath practice, but it is more than that. *Pranayama*, as it is best understood, is the movement of God-breath, of spirit, in our being. It can be used to energize or calm, depending on the breath pattern that is practiced. But no matter the pattern, it is in the *attention* that we bring to our breath, that we find our strength and spirit. It is in being mindful of our breath, that breath and spirit combine and transform into Holy Breathing.

BREATH PRAYER

Inhale ◆ Ru-

Exhale ◆ ach

POSE FOCUS This week, take your yoga practice off your mat. Select a day, set a timer, and every few hours throughout the day pause and intentionally take three full, slow breaths. Note the many different places where you can pause and, with awareness, breathe: in the car, at the office, while doing dishes, or in line at the grocery store. Don't worry about doing it "right"; bring no expectations of spiritual presence but simply take the time throughout one day to bring attention to your breath and observe yourself doing so. Be like the earth: inhale God.

The Practice of Healthy Self Love

SCRIPTURE Keep your heart with all vigilance,
for from it flow the springs of life.
PROVERBS 4:23

SPIRITUAL FOCUS "Not only do self-love and love of others
go hand in hand but ultimately they are indistinguishable."
M. SCOTT PECK

DEVOTION The book of Proverbs is probably the best self-help book ever written. It does not delineate laws we must follow in order to attain a higher status in God's eyes (as though we could do so or God would require us to); instead, it points out paths that will lead us to healthy and holy living. One important lesson the proverbs teach us is that it is only when we exercise self-control that we will come to understand how to achieve healing and wholeness, to recognize God's love for us.

Self-control is an integral practice of yoga. The yoga concept of *brahmacharya* is a discipline of self-control that leads to a moral life. The term, which translates literally as *"walk with God,"* is an invitation to see the sacred in everyday living—to fully and consciously BE ourselves. Yoga and scripture intersect in teaching us that we engage a mature sense of our authentic self by learning that self-love flows from God and may be accessed through the practice of self-control.

Another way to practice healthy self-love is to try to see yourself through the eyes of those people in the world who really love you. There is a tribe in South Africa that practices an unusual form of love for people who have acted criminally. They bring these individuals to the center of their town and for two days repeatedly tell them from a positive stance how they view them . . . how they love them. The outcome is often that the person begins to learn both about forgiveness and about self-love. In his "greatest commandment" (his concise summation of the spirit of the original ten), Jesus says, *"Love God . . .* and love your neighbor as yourself." Loving God is a given for the believer, but to love our neighbor is impossible if we don't first love ourselves.

BREATH PRAYER

Inhale ◆ Keep

Exhale ◆ My Heart

POSE FOCUS *Savasana*, Corpse pose, is one of the few requirements, besides breath-centered movement, of a yoga *asana* practice. *Savasana* is yoga's quintessential restorative pose, but it is much more than that. *Savasana* "seals the deal" at the end of the practice, creating time and space for the lessons learned in practice to be absorbed, whether consciously or unconsciously. If only one pose can be practiced, the yogi elders advise, "*let it be savasana.*" This week make this ancient wisdom your own. Pick a time and place outside your yoga class or home practice to just practice *savasana*. To prevent the exercise from turning into a nap, bring your breath to the practice. Watch your inhalation and exhalation and bring your attention back to your breath whenever your mind wanders. Absorb the lessons surrounding you.

The Practice of Being Happy and Holy

SCRIPTURE Base your happiness on your hope in Christ.
ROMANS 12:12 *PHILLIPS*

SPIRITUAL FOCUS "What a happy and holy fashion it is that those who love one another should rest on the same pillow."
NATHANIEL HAWTHORNE

DEVOTION At a recent Yogadevotion spring retreat a conversation ensued among participants about the title of the retreat: Happy AND Holy. The idea that one could be happy and holy at the same time was at the center of the dialogue. It wasn't hard for participants to visualize happiness as a faithful follower of the ways of Jesus, but many struggled to see holiness as part of their interior story. God is holy, Jesus is holy, and the Spirit is holy, but do we see ourselves as fitting that description?

Sometimes, in an attempt to wrap our minds around certain concepts we engage in an either/or narrative: we or they, in or out, happy or holy? But these are false dichotomies; Richard Rohr refers to this kind of thought pattern as "dualistic" thinking. In Jesus' language there is no "or"; there is only love. When we are able to look through the lens of love we see no other possible scenario: all are truly welcome, and holiness naturally follows our happiness.

One of the best things going on in the yoga world right now is the idea that yoga is for EVERYbody. This has always been the case, but it has taken a while for EVERYbody to embrace this truth. You may hear a reminder from a yoga teacher that goes something like this: "*Modifications in* asana *are neither lesser nor better; they are simply the same pose, done differently.*" Chair yoga is for EVERY body, and adaptive yoga is a powerful practice.

The interconnectedness between happiness and holiness is a faith practice we can take away from our mats. When we connect with God's Holy Spirit, draw upon the love God has so freely given us, and share that love into the world as happy AND holy people, we change the narratives that have divided us.

BREATH PRAYER

Inhale ◆ I Am

Exhale ◆ Happy AND Holy

POSE FOCUS Twists are a wonderful way to embody the concept of "and" rather than "or." As we rotate the spine we both compress and stretch, stimulate and sooth. Whether standing, seated, or supine, always begin your twist with a gentle contraction of the belly on an exhalation. This engages the torso first, allowing the twist to emanate from the spine rather than from the shoulders or neck. Upon inhalation lengthen your spine, chest open, and on the subsequent exhalation you might find more room in the twist. Breathe easily and steadily while holding the pose. When one direction is completed, embrace the other.

The Practice of Longing and Belonging

SCRIPTURE God has given us the task of telling everyone what he is doing. We're Christ's representatives. God uses us to persuade men and women to drop their differences and enter into God's work of making things right between them. We're speaking for Christ himself now: Become friends with God; he's already a friend with you.

2 CORINTHIANS 5:17–20 *THE MESSAGE*

SPIRITUAL FOCUS "Longing, felt fully, carries us to belonging."

TARA BRACH

DEVOTION We are all longing to belong. We don't long to belong to just anything; we long to belong to Love with a capital *L*. We take detours away from this Love sometimes—possibly many times—in an attempt to figure things out, yet we're always welcome to come home to Love. Thanks be to God that God is faithful to the promise to be with us always, no matter what, that God always stands ready to guide us back home through the gentle nudges of the Holy Spirit. God fulfilled the promise of belonging in Jesus, and when we live the way of Jesus—the way of peace, harmony, love, and care for neighbor as our self—we capture the essence of what it means to long, belong, and live.

In yoga we have a Sanskrit word for "community"—*sangha*, which implies that we belong to each other for support. "Tribe" is another word for "community," the difference being that it carries the weight of survival in its meaning, whereas *sangha* is more about community support and awakening. We live out our faith through our yoga practice when we embrace the idea that what we do on the mat is reflected in our actions off the mat and in community. In our faith practices we understand that we belong to God and to each other for the sake of our world . . . the world that God loved so much that God sent Jesus to show us how to live together in love.

BREATH PRAYER

Inhale ◆ I Am

Exhale ◆ a Friend

POSE FOCUS You might not think so, but living in community takes practice. This week practice community on and off your mat. Take a class, arrange to meet a friend and practice yoga together, or perhaps bring your mat to a public park where you know others practice. Practice community off your mat as well. Bring extra homegrown produce to a local food pantry, show up for a community service project, or organize a neighborhood block party. However you choose to practice community, bring to the practice your full presence and attention and suspend judgment of your neighbors. Be a friend.

The Practice of Showing Up

SCRIPTURE "I go to prepare a place for you, . . . and if I go and prepare a place for you, I will come again and will take you to myself, so that where I am, there you may be also."

JOHN 14:2-3

SPIRITUAL FOCUS "Eighty percent of success is showing up."

WOODY ALLEN

DEVOTION A young woman quietly sneaks into class during the opening breath work, rolls out her mat, and sits down. The same young woman barely makes it to church in time to hear the sermon and always sits in the back pew. During the open sharing of peace at the beginning of class, she was overheard to say, *"Sometimes it is all I can do to just show up."*

Life is like that sometimes. There can be so many obstacles that attempt to keep us from being in relationship with the One who loves us, multiple reasons that prevent us from practicing our faith or yoga. Sometimes the explanation is as straightforward as that we're too tired, or perhaps other priorities have pushed their way to the top of the "to do" list. But when we press through and simply commit to showing up, in whatever circumstance we find ourselves, we will be surprised to find that God has gone before and has prepared a place for us.

BREATH PRAYER

Inhale ◆ I Am

Exhale ◆ Here

POSE FOCUS I know of no quicker method for bringing my attention to the present, for "showing up" on the mat, than practicing balance poses. In this week's practice add an extra balance pose. Tree and Warrior III are examples of two familiar favorites. In balance poses we begin by finding a focus; pick a spot at which to direct your eye gaze or *drishti,* and bring your mind's attention to your breath, keeping it full and steady. Ground the pose with your feet and pull energy from the earth up into your body, engaging the core as the spine lengthens. Show up and find balance.

The Practice of Returning

SCRIPTURE For thus said the Lord God, the Holy One of Israel:
In returning and rest you shall be saved;
in quietness and in trust shall be your strength.

ISAIAH 30:15

SPIRITUAL FOCUS "There is nothing like returning
to a place that remains unchanged to find the ways
in which you yourself have altered."

NELSON MANDELA

DEVOTION "Welcome back" is a theme we see at almost every turn this time of the year. Welcome back to school, to church. Welcome back to new rhythms at work and in life. For those returning to faith and yoga practices there is a renewed sense of strength in community, and for those new to such practice there is the wonder of new beginnings.

Our Scripture this week is an invitation to the people of Israel and to us to return to God and rest. The passage adds that in returning and finding rest we are saved. The Latin root word for "saved" or "salvation" is *salvus*, which means to be made whole or healed. God's repeated invitation to return, to rest in quietness, and to renew and restore our strength is an invitation to heal, to be made whole. In Yogadevotion we learn to rest in God by practicing in God's presence. Through movement, breath, devotion, and prayer we celebrate that in God we are **always** welcomed back.

BREATH PRAYER

Inhale ◆ I Am

Exhale ◆ Back

POSE FOCUS Whether standing or seated, we return again and again in practice to Mountain pose, *tadasana*. It provides the centered grounding we need to check in with our breath and body. This week, return to practicing Mountain pose. Root your feet into the earth and stack your joints to align your body: knees over ankles, hips over knees, and shoulders over hips. Notice your breath and rest in the quiet strength of the pose.

The Practice of De-cluttering

SCRIPTURE Do what is fair and just to your neighbor,
be compassionate and loyal in your love,
and don't take yourself too seriously—
take God seriously.
MICAH 6:8 *THE MESSAGE*

SPIRITUAL FOCUS "Clutter isn't just in your home, attic,
garage or office. Clutter is also in your mind, and distracts
you from the amazing things you were meant to do."
KATRINA MAYER

DEVOTION There are certain predictable times in our lives when we experience an innate urge to clear out "stuff" we no longer need. Most of us hold on to life's trappings longer than necessary, and it takes up space: physically, emotionally and spiritually. De-cluttering is one way for us to create space, preparing us for something new, something different. We typically de-clutter when we move out of our family home as young adults to prepare to live independently. Reorganizing a home before a child is born is a way to welcome a new life. We also de-clutter as we age, preparing to transition or downsize our physical accumulations.

Sometimes our mind is so "stuffed" that we hold on to old ways of thinking, even in terms of our faith, and miss out on the new things God is up to in our life. De-cluttering the inner closet of our mind begins with the question *What does God require of me?* Our Yogadevotion practice is a great place to ask those questions: What *is* required of me: of my body, my mind, my spirit? De-cluttering the inner closet of our mind reveals God-space in our life and shows us that, at the center, all God requires of us is love—love for God, our neighbor, and ourselves.

BREATH PRAYER

Inhale ◆ I Am

Exhale ◆ Love

POSE FOCUS We strengthen our love with heart-opening poses. Try incorporating cactus or goal post arms with a variety of poses this week. Elbows are bent at 90 degrees, level with our shoulders. We gently squeeze together our shoulder blades, allowing our chest to expand and our heart to lead the body. With practice our de-cluttered mind learns to follow our heart.

The Practice of Accommodating Failure

SCRIPTURE Jesus said, "Come ahead." Jumping out of the boat, Peter walked on the water to Jesus. But when he looked down at the waves churning beneath his feet, he lost his nerve and started to sink. He cried, "Master, save me!"

MATTHEW 14:29–30 *THE MESSAGE*

SPIRITUAL FOCUS "Success is not final, failure is not fatal: it is the courage to continue that counts."

WINSTON CHURCHILL

DEVOTION Pause for a moment and remember a time when you tried something new and felt overwhelmed. Listening carefully to the teacher, you thought you had a handle on things, but then it became too much. At the root of your anxiety was the fear of failure. Frequently after a first yoga class a new student will come up and say, "There is so much to remember, and I'm sure I'm not doing it right!" A felt need to do "it" right is part of our DNA; we are taught to avoid failure. But the truth is that when we fail we open ourselves up to the opportunity of learning something new.

Stepping out of our comfort zone, risking failure, is the place where head and heart meet and we are most open. Stepping out of our comfort zone does not mean for us to invite injury by doing something our body knows is unsafe. But risking failure may mean taking a yoga class for the first time. Failure might even look like taking the opportunity to rest in a given pose while the remainder of the class moves on, even if it may look to others as though we can't "do" the pose. Be assured that such a choice is an example of courage and wisdom, not failure.

Brené Brown in her book *Rising Strong* points out that it is when we fail, when we are face down in the muck and mire of life, that we often get our greatest inspiration in terms of how to move ahead. Accommodating failure in our yoga practice and in our life takes courage and wisdom, and it teaches us about trust. It was only when Peter trained his gaze and focus on Jesus, trusting him, that he stepped out without fear. When Peter looked down he fell, he failed, . . . and he learned. Peter's failure to focus taught him that he could trust Jesus with his life. With wisdom and courage we accept that we might fail—trusting that this very failure will provide an opportunity to plot a new course.

BREATH PRAYER

Inhale ◆ I Trust

Exhale ◆ in the Lord

POSE FOCUS Pick two balance poses and practice transitioning from one to the other. Perhaps you will transition from Tree to Airplane balance (Warrior III variation with arms along side the body). Find your focus and then transition from one balance pose to the next on an exhalation, keeping your core strong and your belly gently contracted; then inhale the spine long into the next pose. Notice where your mind and gaze is during the transition, as well as where it is if you fall out of the pose. You may learn something!

The Practice of Restoring

SCRIPTURE We don't just put up with our limitations; we celebrate them, and then go on to celebrate every strength, every triumph of the truth in you. We pray hard that it will all come together in our lives.

2 CORINTHIANS 13:9 *THE MESSAGE*

SPIRITUAL FOCUS "Initially, when I first became a Christian and got into ministry, my thought was that God existed to make my life better and to take me to Heaven. Now I realize that it is not about me at all. It is all about God and . . . [God's] plan to restore the Earth to the Garden of Eden."

MAX LUCADO

DEVOTION Returning to our mats or to any situation we haven't visited for a while can bring us face-to-face with our limitations. Stepping back onto our mats, we find new muscles and perhaps changes in our joints or mobility. Coming back to a situation from which we've been away promises to bring changes: some welcome, while others may be disappointing. Yoga and faith practices teach us that when we hit places of limitation— physically, emotional or spiritually—we can find new strength in God's promise to restore us to wholeness, to heal us in body, mind, and spirit.

The word *restore* has its root in a medical term that means literally to put back in joint, to come together. We find strength when we are put back together in a new way that remembers our original state of being. In yoga we practice restoration by adapting an *asana* to accommodate something that doesn't feel right in our bodies. In faith restoration we might reexamine some long held belief that has changed or developed based upon new information and life experiences.

In today's reading the apostle Paul goes a step further, urging us to *celebrate* our limitations because the restoration is God's work—and God's work is always a cause for celebration. Whether or not we are at that place of celebrating our areas of weakness—and most of us are not— we're promised that our limitations do not have the ultimate authority. When we celebrate our humanness we see our situation through a different lens. We see a new path, a path that moves us beyond our perceived limits. God put us back together, restored—for our sake and for the sake of our life together. This is both our reality and our prayer!

BREATH PRAYER

Inhale ◆ Restore Me

Exhale ◆ Oh Lord

POSE FOCUS Choose a restorative pose to revisit—perhaps one such as *supta baddha konasana*—supine butterfly—that brings your limitations to the fore. Pause for a moment before beginning the pose to ask yourself *What do I feel? Could I relax more if my knees were supported with blankets? Does my lower back feel pinched?* Perhaps this pose would be more effective if done sitting. Acknowledge your limitations, make adjustments, come into your breath, and find comfort and ease in the pose. Restore.

The Practice of Avoiding Ditches

SCRIPTURE Jesus said, "I am the way,
and the truth, and the life."
JOHN 14:6

SPIRITUAL FOCUS "Love is the bridge
between you and everything."
RUMI

DEVOTION Have you ever been asked a question about your vision of some future event? You describe your thought, and your companion's response indicates that he or she clearly does not understand your idea. For example, you might say, "I'd like to see more diversity in our schools," and the person with whom you are in conversation responds, "I'm against quotas!" This is an example of jumping from one ditch to another, going from one side to the other and completely missing the point.

Our engagement with Jesus' words in John 14:6 often suffers from the same kind of disconnect, and we too easily miss the point. When Jesus says "I Am the way, the truth and the life," he is speaking about *the way he has taught us to live*. One of those ways—as radically divergent from the norm in his day as it is in ours—is to choose the path of peace. At the fifteenth anniversary Ground Zero prayer service each of the major world religions was asked to prepare a meditation on peace. Jewish, Muslim, Hindu, B'ahi, Greek Orthodox, Christian—all came together and through their meditations jointly proclaimed a path of peace as the way we are to live. The prayer service closed with the song "Let There Be Peace on Earth." This familiar hymn has the power to remind us of our own role in bringing peace to this world, the power to draw us out of the ditches into which we easily slip and get us back onto the path.

Let peace begin with us—on our mats, in our homes, on the job, and in the world. The way of peace Jesus taught calls on us to take the high road and avoid the ditches.

BREATH PRAYER

Inhale ◆ Let Peace

Exhale ◆ Begin with Me

POSE FOCUS Bridge pose, *Setu Bandha Sarvangasana*, is often used as a transitional pose to re-align the spine. This week practice Bridge pose with the shoulders *flat* on the mat, and press the feet into the mat as the hips are gently lifted. Relax the glutes, and notice that the strength of the grounded shoulders and feet allows the heart energy to rise—bridging over a ditch.

The Practice of Being Grounded

SCRIPTURE Then shall all the trees of the forest sing for joy before the LORD.

1 CHRONICLES 16:33

SPIRITUAL FOCUS "The only trees that survive hurricanes are the ones that have deep roots and supple strength to bend with the winds of the storm."

BARON BAPTISTE

DEVOTION Deep roots and supple strength . . . it is hardly a surprise that those who seem to weather the storms of life and still find joy are people who are grounded. They don't panic easily, they are flexible, and they seem to have a sense or confidence that "everything is going to be all right."

In our yoga practice we build our asanas from the foundation up. We ground down to gain stability and balance before we go further into the pose. In our faith practice we are rooted in God's promise of everlasting presence and life. Our foundation is based not in our own strength but in God's promise. Deeply rooted and possessing supple strength, we are free to grow and revel in the joy of The Lord—no matter the weather.

BREATH PRAYER

Inhale ◆ I Sing

Exhale ◆ Before the Lord

POSE FOCUS Tree pose, *vriksa-sana*, is one of the iconic yoga *asanas*, and yogis have lots of advice on how best to enter the pose. This week, keep it simple. Get back to your roots—maybe practice a modified, so-called "simpler" version so that the focus is on the foundation of the pose: grounding down to lift up. Then spread your branches and sway in the breeze.

The Practice of Pilgrimage

SCRIPTURE In all your ways acknowledge [God],
and [God] will make straight your paths.
PROVERBS 3:6

SPIRITUAL FOCUS "Profound joy of the heart is like
a magnet that indicates the path of life."
MOTHER TERESA

DEVOTION A PBS special, "A Path Will Appear," was the topic of an overheard conversation at a coffee shop. What does it mean that a path will appear? The documentary was about people who felt disconnected from the faith in which they had been brought up (or from religion in general) but had gone on pilgrimage because they still felt called to something greater than themselves. It was while they were on pilgrimage that a path appeared connecting their head with their heart and enabling them to experience the Holy.

Jesus understood that people need different ways in which to hear the Good News of God's unconditional love, so he taught through signs and wonders, healing, lectures, public discourse, prayer, and retreat. He taught in many ways so that each person could experience God along his or her unique path. A faith-based yoga practice creates sacred space and may be one way to lead people to experience the Holy, to travel back to God. We are all on a journey, a pilgrimage of faith. When we find space in our busy lives to be open ourselves to God's presence, to acknowledge God in our lives, we too will glimpse a path.

BREATH PRAYER

Inhale ◆ God

Exhale ◆ in Me

POSE FOCUS I love the straight lines of Five Pointed Star—a *trikonasana* variation. Stand with feet wide apart, weight evenly distributed and knees soft. Press into the ground with your feet, and on inhalation lift your arms up and out to the side, or shoulder height, as you lengthen your spine. Breathe into the pose and feel your heart opening as your limbs extend straight and long.

The Practice of Instilled Peace

SCRIPTURE God is not a God of disorder but of peace.
1 CORINTHIANS 14:33

SPIRITUAL FOCUS "Peace does not mean to be in a place where there is no noise, trouble or hard work. It means to be in the midst of those things and still be calm in your heart."
AUTHOR UNKNOWN

DEVOTION Peace is a matter of the heart. Giving and receiving, sharing the peace, is a first step toward visualizing what peace could look like when practiced in our chaotic world. When we watch the world through the lens of the nightly news, when we experience chaos in our own or another person's life, we are moved to search for a place of stability, order, and peace. The peace for which we yearn is indwelling, infused within us by a loving God. Instilled peace moves us from the notion of peace as an isolated, disconnected expression to an established way of living.

Recognizing the peace within our self and carrying that peace into our everyday life takes practice. But when we practice instilled peace we are able to extract order from chaos—in essence experiencing God's very nature. In our yoga faith practice we use the time on our mats to experience peace in our calming breath and slowing heart rate, inviting us to reconnect with God's promise of order drawn from chaos. This is a practice that lives off the mat and into the world, so that when we feel God's peaceful imprint upon our heart we are enabled to extend God's peace out into the world.

Peace BE with you.

BREATH PRAYER

Inhale ◆ Peace in Me

Exhale ◆ Peace in You

POSE FOCUS Seated Forward Fold, *pashimottanasana*, can be one of yoga's most calming *asanas*. Practice it this week, whether from a chair or on a mat with knees soft and with a calming *langhana* breath—extending your exhalation relative to your inhalation. Enter into the pose with an even breath count. Perhaps your breath count will proceed in this manner: two-count inhalation followed by a four-count exhalation, three-count inhalation followed by a six-count exhalation, and so on, until you find your deepest exhalation. Breathe with steadiness and comfort, and sink deeper into the pose with each exhalation, savoring God's peace.

The Practice of Abundance

SCRIPTURE On the third day there was a wedding in Cana of Galilee, and the mother of Jesus was there. Jesus and his disciples had also been invited to the wedding. When the wine gave out, the mother of Jesus said to him, "They have no wine." . . . His mother said to the servants, "Do whatever he tells you."

JOHN 2:1–3, 5

SPIRITUAL FOCUS "Abundance is not something we acquire, it is something we tune into."

WAYNE DYER

DEVOTION Sitting around a table over a cup of coffee, a conversation broke out among friends about *how much is enough?* The question was prompted by one who was planning to work indefinitely because he didn't think he'd ever have enough to feel comfortable retiring. As his story unfolded it became clear that he had lived with meager resources at some point in his life and never wanted to go back there. No amount of money would make him feel secure. He had developed a condition known as an *abundance block*—you may know it as a scarcity mentality—that prevented him from tuning in to the abundance that was all around him.

In the story of the wedding at Cana, we often focus on Jesus' first miracle: the abundance of fine wine produced from plain water. But it might surprise us to recognize, when we listen closely a second time to the whole story, that there is abundance throughout. We see it in Mary's radical hospitality. The mother of Jesus intervenes and as a result changes the outcome of what would have been an irremediable faux pas for the wedding party: running out of wine. We see the abundance of faith Mary had in her son to remedy the situation. And, as noted, we see Jesus respond abundantly, providing a profusion of the finest wine with which to satiate all the guests.

In the yoga world we have an ethical observance, a *niyama*, called *santosha*—the practice of contentment. To be content with the plenty that surrounds us, we must first recognize it. But our faith-based yoga practice teaches us to take *santosha* a step further: when we tune in to God's abundant nature we come to understand abundance as something to be shared. Sharing our multiplicity of blessings, our abundance, (no matter what form they take) with our neighbor increases both their contentment and our own.

BREATH PRAYER

Inhale ◆ I Am

Exhale ◆ Content

POSE FOCUS Sunflower flow, a variation of *utkata konasana*, is a joyful *asana*. Start with legs wide, feet turned out, arms reaching upward as though to gather light from heaven. On an exhalation bend your knees (they remain over your ankles) as you drop your bottom and circle your arms down to gather up your harvest from the earth. Your back stays long and straight. On an inhalation circle your arms back up toward heaven as you straighten your legs. Enjoy the abundance of light and earth energies that awake during this flowing *asana*.

The Practice of Praise

SCRIPTURE Great is the LORD, and greatly to be praised; his greatness is unsearchable.

PSALM 145:3

SPIRITUAL FOCUS "The highest form of worship is the (practice) of unselfish Christian service. The greatest form of praise is the sound of consecrated feet seeking out the lost and helpless."

REV. BILLY GRAHAM

DEVOTION *Hallelujah* is an ancient word derived from the Hebrew language. *Halla* means to praise, and *Jah* or *Yah* is one name for God. In church, praise and worship often take the form of singing hymns or reciting prayers—many of which contain the word *Hallelujah*. But no matter the words, praise and worship are *acts* of adoration for the One who has created and loves us. A lovely physical way to express our adoration of God is to close our eyes and fold our hands, as we were taught as children.

Fr. Tom Ryan, CSP, author of *Prayer of Heart and Body: Meditation and Yoga as Christian Spiritual Practice*, teaches that every movement of hands and feet, eye gaze and breath, set with an intention to adore God, is an act of praise and worship. Yogadevotion has embraced this belief since its inception.

When we raise our hands, looking toward the heavens, or ground down through our feet, connecting with the earth with an intention to praise God, we are engaged in worship. When we take what we learn in praising God off the mat and into the world, we participate in the ultimate manifestation of worship: loving and caring for our neighbor. Hallelujah!

BREATH PRAYER

Inhale ◆ Halle-

Exhale ◆ lujah!

POSE FOCUS *Surya Namaskara*, Sun Salutation, is one of the most recognized *asana* sequences in yoga. This week make this familiar sequence, a practice of praise to the Creator. You might decide to practice the *asana* with breath, while repeating a favorite prayer such as the Lord's Prayer. For example, start in Mountain pose. Inhale as you raise your arms overhead to "*Our Father who art in heaven*." Next, exhale to Standing Forward Fold, arms circling downward, on "*hallowed be thy name*." You get the idea. Combining praise with your practice transforms it, revealing a pathway to God's healing love. Hallelujah!

The Practice of Coming Home

SCRIPTURE "Those who love me will keep my word, and my Father will love them, and we will come to them and make our home with them."

JOHN 14:23

SPIRITUAL FOCUS "It's a funny thing coming home. Nothing changes. Everything looks the same, feels the same, smells the same. You realize what's changed is you."

F. SCOTT FITZGERALD

DEVOTION All Saints Day is a church holiday that people across the world observe in a variety of interesting ways, from floating candles in a moonlit pond to the simple act of laying a wreath at a grave. But no matter the practice, the intention is to remember those saints who have gone before us to the next realm. For people who have lost a cherished someone, hearing the name of their loved one spoken aloud in church, in memorial, is like coming home to their own faith story.

Yet coming home can also be difficult, despite the many holiday TV commercials that would suggest otherwise. Sometimes coming home reminds us too painfully of why we left in the first place. Sometimes coming home causes feelings of loss to resurface—grief for those we have loved and lost or even a wistful yearning for the way things "used to be."

In yoga we come home to our bodies by practicing Presence. We pay attention to how our body feels in each pose. We appreciate what our body can—in distinction from what it cannot, or can no longer—do. We look for the Presence of God that surrounds us—in times of ease and difficulty, joy and sorrow. Our faith and yoga practices show us that it is sufficient to simply be present to the One who loves us enough to make a home in our heart.

BREATH PRAYER

Inhale ◆ I Have Arrived

Exhale ◆ I Am Home

POSE FOCUS *Sthira and Sukha*, steadiness and ease, are basic tenets of yoga practice. We bring Presence to our practice and give our busy "monkey" minds something to do by assessing each pose. *Is my breath even and deep? Is my body steady and comfortable? Is my attention on my pose?* This week bring *sthira and sukha* to your practice: come home to your body without judgment, arrive in the pose with breath, fully present. BE.

The Practice of Saying Grace

SCRIPTURE Those who observe the day, observe it in honor of the Lord. Also those who eat, eat in honor of the Lord, since they give thanks to God.

ROMANS 14:6

SPIRITUAL FOCUS "You say grace before meals. All right. But I say grace before the concert and the opera, and grace before the play and pantomime, and grace before I open a book, and grace before sketching, painting, swimming, fencing, boxing, walking, playing, dancing and grace before I dip the pen in the ink."

G. K. CHESTERTON

DEVOTION Saying grace is a spiritual practice defined as returning thanks to God, who has given humanity dominion over all the earth, in part for the cultivation of crops and the procurement of food. Many faith traditions share this practice. In the Lutheran tradition a grace is spoken both before and after the meal. Before the meal the wording is, "*Come, Lord Jesus, be our guest. May these gifts to us be blessed,*" while the after meal grace, from Psalm 136:1, affirms our gratitude: "*O give thanks unto the LORD, for He is good: For His mercy endures forever.*"

In the coming week people across our land will bow their heads and give thanks, either spoken aloud or in the unspoken language of the heart. We will give thanks for food, for family, and for God's providence. In saying grace we will invite God's Presence to be at home with us, to be our guest in all circumstances. How much stronger that invitation becomes when we say grace in community, affirming our gratitude with a resounding *Amen!*

Inviting God to be our guest, whether this takes place at the table or on our mats, empowers us to face any event or life experience. Saying grace acknowledges God as Creator and Provider of all that is good.

And all God's children say "*Amen*"!

BREATH PRAYER

Inhale ◆ Aa-a-a-

Exhale ◆ men!

POSE FOCUS *Anjali Mudra,* Prayer pose, is literally translated "honor" or "celebrate." How apt a description for a hand position commonly used to celebrate the Lord's goodness to us as we say grace! Each day this week invite Prayer pose into your practice in a new way. You might consider using prayer hands as you transition from Mountain pose to standing Forward Fold. Or perhaps you might use prayer hands in Bridge pose, affirming the lifting of your heart with the placement of your hands. Wherever you insert prayer hands into your practice, observe the space that it creates in the underlying pose. Maybe, there will be enough space for an extra *Amen!*

The Practice of Gratitude

SCRIPTURE We [are] satisfied with the goodness
of your house, your holy temple.
By awesome deeds you answer us with
deliverance, O God of our salvation.

PSALM 65:4–5

SPIRITUAL FOCUS "Paying attention to what we feel
grateful for puts us in a positive frame of mind. It connects
us to the world around us and to ourselves."

LISA FIRESTONE

DEVOTION This past weekend many of us experienced a slow, intentional movement from verbalized praise and thanksgiving, spoken words of grace around a table, to a quiet, unspoken profusion of gratitude. One Yogadevotion instructor acknowledged that this year she had simply rested in gratitude, feeling no compulsion to rush the Thanksgiving celebration. She had decided that, rather than putting up her Christmas tree as soon as the leftovers and dishes from the feast had been put away, she was going to wait, sit in gratitude, and enjoy this time, paying attention to the foci of her gratitude.

We enter a season that invites us into the story of the people of Israel. We join them in spirit during their protracted wait for the promised Savior. As people who have entered the story of the Christ Child, we wait in gratitude each year for the story to be retold. Basking in quiet gratitude is a great way to begin listening for the story of how God permeated human history, coming in human form to dwell among us in tangible realization of the long-awaited promise of Presence. Because of the story we approach our practice in gratitude for hope fulfilled.

BREATH PRAYER

Inhale ◆ I Am

Exhale ◆ Grateful

POSE FOCUS *Sukasana*, Easy pose, is a pose from childhood: sitting crossed-legged on the floor. As adults we find Easy pose to be a great hip opener, but it can also present challenges to knees and tight pelvis muscles. This week find your variation of Easy pose, whether on the floor, sitting on a cushion or block, or perhaps seated in a chair. The pose requires only that you sit still and tall. Once your have found your comfortable seat, ask yourself two questions: (1) *What impediment that no longer serves me can I get rid of in this pose?* and (2) *Where did I see the Holy today?* Listen to your answers and release into gratitude.

The Practice of an Authentic Attitude

SCRIPTURE "Come, let us go up to the mountain of the Lord, to the house of the God of Jacob; that he may teach us his ways and that we may walk in his paths."
ISAIAH 2:3

SPIRITUAL FOCUS "Choosing the right path is seldom easy. It is a decision we make with only our hearts to guide us."
AUTHOR UNKNOWN

DEVOTION *Advent*, which means "coming" in Latin, is typically a season of waiting, listening, and preparing to celebrate the mystery of God with us, Immanuel. It is also a season that challenges our sense of well-BEing, however, as often, and on many levels, it catches us overDOing. Cultivating a right attitude about the days leading up to the holidays will help us stay true to our authentic self, our true nature as people who have heard the sacred teachings and are walking the path.

Yoga brings awareness of more than our bodies through the *asanas*; it attunes us to our thoughts, which in turn shape our attitudes. In our faith-based yoga practice we cultivate an openness to encounter God, both on our mats and in the larger world—and this encounter will shape our attitudes toward life and lead us to recognize our true nature as children of God. The invitation to cultivate an authentic life attitude this holiday season deflects our presence away from DOing toward the infinitely more fulfilling path of hope, peace, joy, and love.

BREATH PRAYER

Inhale ◆ Walk

Exhale ◆ with Me

POSE FOCUS Have you ever noticed that the set of a person's head and shoulders denotes their attitude: submissive, belligerent, hopeful, or depressed? The neck is the key to our head/shoulder alignment. This week in practice pay attention to your neck, seeking ease and comfort for it in each pose. Strengthen neck alignment by practicing Locust pose, or *salabhasana*. Lie on your belly, arms alongside your body. On inhalation lift your chest, heart center, forward and upward as you lift both legs off the mat. Keep the back of your neck long—continuous with the spine. Upon exhalation lower your chest and legs down to the mat, turning your head so that your *right* cheek rests on the ground. On the next inhalation bring the head back to center as you lift the chest and legs. Then on the next exhalation lower to the mat, resting your *left* cheek on the ground. Continue for several rounds, feeling the strength of your upper back as you lift and allowing your neck to turn and then relax as you lower to the mat.

The Practice of Patient Waiting

SCRIPTURE Those who wait for the LORD shall renew their strength, they shall mount up with wings like eagles.

ISAIAH 40:31

SPIRITUAL FOCUS "A waiting person is a patient person. The word patience means the willingness to stay where we are and live the situation out to the full in belief that something hidden there will manifest itself to us."

HENRI J. M. NOUWEN

DEVOTION Every parent and teacher knows how hard it is to wait for a child to perform some task. It is so tempting to intervene, to do it for them. But in order to learn, children must be given a chance to follow through on their own. The struggle to wait patiently reveals something about our human nature. We are regularly pressed by society to "*get 'er done,*" and under this pressure we may choose a hasty response, deceiving ourselves into the assumption that this is better than none at all. Not surprisingly, those knee-jerk responses often lack wisdom, and we regret having made them. The truth is that when we are patient—at times it may seem excruciatingly so—we demonstrate love, trust, and an investment in what we are waiting for.

In this season of waiting we are invited to be countercultural. Rather than rushing in to a decision or conclusion, we are invited to wait for the Spirit of the Lord to lead us. Elizabeth waited in hope for many years for the birth of her son, John the Baptist. For a nine-month period that may have seemed equally as long, Mary waited in peace, pondering her seemingly bizarre circumstances after the angel had informed her that she would bear a child and name him Jesus. And Jesus waited throughout his three-year ministry for humanity to "catch up" with his message of love.

The faith practice of waiting is intrinsically connected to our ability to trust God. The yoga practice of waiting is similar: we are called to wait in a breath or pose, to trust our bodies to give us information on how, or if, we are to proceed or back off. These cues from our mind/body connection keep us safe and teach us how to accurately perceive both our limitations and our areas of strength. Waiting patiently while trusting God leads us into a mature experience of who we are as physical, emotional, and spiritual beings. Time and time again we find that when we patiently wait the Lord renews our strength, enabling us to rise up as though on the wings of eagles.

BREATH PRAYER

Inhale ◆ I

Exhale ◆ Will Wait

POSE FOCUS Eagle pose, *garudasana*, challenges our patience—with our balance, with our flexibility, with our strength, and with ourselves. This week, approach Eagle pose with patience; take it in steps and investigate the many alternative positions for arms and legs progressively, starting with the simplest variations and avoiding any position that causes joint pain. Find your own version of Eagle: one that allows you to wait patiently in the pose, deepen your breath, and *soar*.

The Practice of Radiating Love

SCRIPTURE [I]n the Lord, [I] beg you to lead a life worthy of the calling to which you have been called, with all humility and gentleness, with patience, bearing with one another in love, making every effort to maintain the unity of the Spirit in the bond of peace.

EPHESIANS 4:1–3

SPIRITUAL FOCUS "Darkness cannot drive out darkness; only light can do that. Hate cannot drive out hate; only love can do that."

MARTIN LUTHER KING JR.

DEVOTION This week we pause to consider a kaleidoscope of faith events. Almost all faith traditions are celebrating a connection with the Sacred this month. Hanukkah commemorates the restoration of the miracle of light in the holy temple of Jerusalem. In pre-Christian Scandinavia the Feast of *Juul*, or Yule, lasting for 12 days, celebrated the rebirth of the sun god and gave rise to the custom of burning a Yule log. After the winter solstice light returns and the days grow incrementally longer. Many traditions pause at this time of year to acknowledge that there is something greater than the self; there is something sacred, and many experience the Sacred in the light that surrounds us.

The Christian faith stands alone in a narrative that celebrates God choosing to become human. It celebrates the story that is proclaimed afresh every Christmas—the story of love coming out of the heavens to dwell among us: of love coming down.

Pastor John Hogenson reframed for many the Christmas narrative when he described God in a single—and then expanded—word: "*Love. Love came down.*" Love came down to show us the way of love, to show us the way of God. The way of Love is wrapped in bands of cloth, kept warm by hay and the steamy breath of livestock. The way of Love that came down more than 2,000 years ago continues to bring hope, peace, and joy to all people, wherever they are on their faith and spiritual journeys. When we light a holiday candle we pause to celebrate Love coming down and driving out hate. We pause to join in unity with all humanity to celebrate One God, for all and in all—to revel in the reality of light driving out darkness.

BREATH PRAYER

Inhale ◆ Love

Exhale ◆ Come Down

POSE FOCUS Consider trying a candle meditation this week. Set a timer for whatever time period you can commit to: perhaps five minutes or twenty. Find a comfortable seat and come into your breath. Repeat to yourself the breath prayer *Love, come down*, or repeat your own sacred word, coordinating the repetition of the word(s) with your breath cycle. When your mind has settled, light your candle and gaze into the flame. Simply watch it dance. If the light is too intense, close your eyes and observe the energy patterns remaining in your internal gaze. Inhale into your being God's white, healing light, and upon exhalation send out the light into the world. Radiate light and love.

The Practice of Hush

SCRIPTURE "Be still, and know that I am God!"
PSALM 46:10

SPIRITUAL FOCUS "Yoga will make you sensitive to the stillness, the presence, the hush, the peace of God. This deep inner stillness is at the core of your being. It is the ground, the joy of your being. The radiant peace you'll experience is what happens naturally when the creative energy of the Universe is allowed to flow through you unobstructed."
ERICH SCHIFFMAN

DEVOTION There is a collective breath that infuses the world the day after Christmas—a breath of hushed stillness, a breath that calls on us to pause, to *hush* and reflect upon that which we have just celebrated, the mystery and miracle of the sacred-human experience. Depending on where you live, the breath of stillness may be ushered in by the silence of a long-awaited snowfall, by a gentle rainfall, or by a steaming cup of cocoa. In the quiet space of remembering the joy of Christmas and looking toward the reordering of our lives in the coming New Year, God invites us to pause and be still, to breathe in God's energy that waits to flow through us.

People of faith and yoga attest that to BE still is one of the hardest contemplative practices. We are trained from early childhood to push forward, to achieve, to DO. Practicing the passive stance of stillness in both magical and ordinary moments is the difference between doing yoga and living yoga, between naming our faith and living our faith. The way of God begins when we deliberately hush, find stillness in mind and body, and open ourselves to experience God's Presence.

BREATH PRAYER

Inhale ◆ I am

Exhale ◆ Still

POSE FOCUS Choose a restorative pose in which to practice stillness. Child's pose, *balasana*, is one of our favorites. Enter the pose with breath, making minor adjustments to get comfortable—and then notice. Bring your awareness first to your body: *What areas are having trouble settling?* Then focus your awareness on your breath: *What is the quality of my breath?* Finally, bring your awareness to your mind: *What thoughts are pulling my attention from the pose?* Name your trouble spots and then gently release them; allow yourself to be absorbed in stillness.

CHAPTER 4

Sample Yogadevotion Class

We are including a description of a sample Yogadevotion class, to further explain how we use the devotions in our yoga practice. This is not a formula. Each of our Yogadevotion teachers inserts the devotions into practice according to the needs of their students and their own creativity as instructors. We encourage you to insert the devotions into your practice in a manner that is most meaningful and beneficial to you. Even if you have only enough time to get on the mat and spend a few minutes with your Breath Prayer, opening to God's presence, you have completed a practice. Follow your heart as you practice, and the way will become clear. In the meantime you might want to try our sample class at home.

Greeting, Centering, and Intention

A Yogadevotion class begins with greeting each other, exchanging the peace. In your home practice this greeting may take the form of ringing a bell to signal that you are beginning your practice or reciting a verse, such as *"This is the day that the Lord has made, let us rejoice and be glad."* However you choose to signal the start of your practice, try repeating it each time you get on your mat. This simple ritual will help your body and mind come to the practice more readily.

Following the greeting we center ourselves and establish an intention for the practice. To center, we bring our attention to our mats, starting in a comfortable position, lying down or sitting, giving ourselves permission to be fully present for the length of the class. It may help to mentally tell ourselves that there *is nowhere else for us to go, nothing else for us to do except to practice and be open to God's presence.* We then notice our breath. At first we just notice it, without trying to control it. When we are fully present to our breath, we read the name of this week's practice—it's the signpost for the practice—and set our practice intention. Keep your intention short and sweet. Our intention is always what we need, here and now.

Scripture, Spiritual Focus, Devotion, and Prayer

Buoyed by our intention, we read the Scripture, the Spiritual Focus, and the Devotion, leaving space to reflect on their meaning in our lives. We conclude this opening of our practice with our Breath Prayer, watching our breath, steady and calm as we deepen our inhalations and exhalations. Perhaps we apply an even count to our breath cycle, inhaling for two counts, exhaling for two counts, inhaling for four counts, exhaling for four counts, etc., until our breath pattern is deep and full.

Pose Focus

Finally, we review the suggested Pose Focus and take a moment to envision how we might incorporate the suggestion into our practice. The suggested Pose Focus does not form a complete practice but rather describes one opportunity to experience the practice theme bodily, through movement and breath. Of course, your personal safety must always inform your physical practice. Listen to the teacher within and assess whether the Pose Focus is available for you to practice safely. If it is not available to your body, perhaps the essence of the practice may be embodied in a different pose of your choosing.

This is not a book about how to do physical yoga. If you need instruction on *asana*, please consult a certified yoga instructor.

The roadmap for the practice is now complete.

Warming Up

We warm up with simple poses, sitting or lying down, that allow us to easily link our breath with movement of the spine. Repeated movements that are synchronized by the breath, followed by short holds, are beneficial to our cold muscles and joints. *Our safety always comes first in our physical practice; our only goal is to link our breath with movement in steadiness and comfort.* We try to prevent competition, expectations, and striving from entering our practice; instead, we seek to fully experience the *asana*, the sensation of the movement, in the form that is right for our body.

Examples of Warm-up Poses:
Gentle Side Bends
Simple Twists
Bridge
Knees to Chest

When we feel sufficiently warmed up, we pause to check in to our bodies, contrasting how we feel now with how we felt when we first got to our mats. We also check in to our intention for the class by becoming still and repeating our Breath Prayer or Sacred Word (see the "Sacred Word" section in Chapter 2) before transitioning to our next sequence.

Standing Poses

In our *vinyasa* flow classes sun salutes and warrior sequences often form the next and most rigorous part of our class. We urge students to use the power of their breath to find the body strength for these large movements. We begin this sequence by grounding down into the earth and drawing the earth's energy up into our bodies through our feet. At the end of the sequence we pause, standing if we are able, and turn our attention to any worries or concerns we may have in our lives. We find that this is a good time to offer up our prayers of healing for our loved ones, the world, and ourselves. With the strength acquired from these poses we come into stillness and synchronize our breath to our prayer offerings, sending out our prayers of healing with our exhalations.

Examples of Standing Poses:
> *Triangle*
> *Extended Side Angle*
> *Warrior I & II*

Balance Postures

We like to include at least two balance postures in our practice. There is nothing like a balance posture to focus your mind and bring your attention to the forefront of your practice. Sometimes balance postures are integrated into our core work as it takes a strong core to balance. Sometimes we use a balance pose to transition poses in our sun salutes and warrior sequences. We begin balance poses by finding our eye gaze focus, our *drishti*. We engage our core as we ground our feet into the earth and lift into our balance posture—well, at least that's what we attempt to do! We try very hard not to judge our balance posture efforts. A good way to let go of judgment is to recite prayer as we balance, using the support of a wall or chair if needed.

Examples of Balance Poses:
> *Tree*
> *Warrior III or Airplane*
> *Dancer*

Seated and Supine Poses

We return to our mats and move into seated and/or supine poses. This is the time for holding a posture in stillness. We like to hold these cooling poses for five full breaths, prolonging our exhalation, sinking a little more deeply into the pose with each exhalation. But we are careful to modify the posture as needed to maintain our personal practice integrity of safety, steadiness, and comfort. We honor our body and inner wisdom by coming out of the posture when we need to.

Examples of Poses include:

Seated Twist
Seated Forward Fold
Supine Spinal Twist

Breath Work, Restorative Poses, and Closing

In classical yoga practices, breath work, or *pranayama,* often comes next. This sequencing helps the body remain energized while moving into restorative poses and/or meditation—so we don't end up taking a nap but are aware and present in the quiet practice. There are many different yogic breathing techniques for moving energy, God Breath, through the body. *Pranayama* should always match the intention of the practice—what is needed by the student. For example, to calm the Spirit, match each slow, full inhalation with a still slower, relaxed exhalation. To bring balance try alternative nostril breathing, *nadi shodhana.* Breath work can be very powerful, but advanced *pranayama* should be attempted only under the guidance of an experienced instructor.

To complete our practice class we assume a restorative posture, settle our bodies into comfort, and come into stillness. We might then repeat the Scripture for this practice. We allow ourselves time in our restorative pose to seal the benefits of the practice into our body, mind, and spirit by bringing our full attention to the effects of the practice, the sensations in our bodies. We give ourselves at least two minutes in this peaceful space, repeating our Breath Prayer or Sacred Word if we are distracted by outside thoughts.

Examples of Restorative Postures:

Savasana
Legs Up the Wall
Supine Butterfly

When we are ready to transition out of our restorative pose, we use our breath to re-energize and move us into a comfortable upright position. If we have a specific meditation practice, now is the time to insert that practice (see below). We close with our hands in prayer position, *anjali mudra*, expressing our gratitude for this time on our mats, thanking our teacher, and committing to take our insights with us out into the world.

Examples of Closing Prayers:

Peace be with you.

The Spirit in me honors the Spirit in you. *Namaste.*

In the name of the Creator, the Son, and the Holy Spirit. Amen.

Peaceful thoughts (prayer hands to your forehead).
Peaceful words (prayer hands to your lips).
Peaceful heart (prayer hands to your heart).

We turn on to our sides and pause to nurture the love of God and the light of Christ that is within each of us; then we reach out and share that love and light with all who are practicing with us and with those whom we remember in the silence of our hearts as we feel the love and light return to us on the breath of the Holy Spirit.

(Hands at heart)
God, open our hearts to love as you first loved us.
(Hands at lips)
Open our mouths to speak words of kindness and compassion to ourselves and to our neighbor.
(Hands at forehead)
May our thoughts be reflected in our actions that witness to the life, the love, and the ministry of Jesus.

Meditation

Our devotional yoga practice is a wonderful way to still the body and mind and connect with the Spirit. But then what? Remaining in that stillness, fully alert and aware in God's presence, is what we call meditation. Many students find meditation to be difficult. Yet to be in stillness, wholly integrated, in full communion with our Creator, can be a profound experience. Sometimes intense emotions, such as grief and sorrow or joy, may arise in this stillness. Most often we experience a few minutes of calm. But it is astounding how much power is in that calm! In calm stillness come clarity and healing. Meditation is a beautiful practice, renowned for its healing effects on the body, mind, and spirit.

Here's one simple meditation practice that can be done in as little as five minutes (you may want to use a timer). Start this meditation at the end of your yoga practice, after restorative poses or *savasana*. It is best to sit up in a comfortable position, well supported, spine long. Take a few full, deep, even-count breaths before meditating to help maintain alertness during the practice.

Begin your meditation by letting go of all the stories running through your mind—stories people tell you and stories you tell yourself. It may help to name your stories as they arise and in so doing put them away on an imagined bookshelf. As you set your stories aside, notice when the story is yours and when it's someone else's. Notice the emotions the stories trigger. You are not trying to stop your thoughts or squelch these internal stories but are merely setting them aside for a short time, to dispassionately observe them without judgment, like a librarian placing a book on a shelf.

If you still find yourself engaged in your mind's narrative, it may help to turn your attention to your breath or repeat your sacred word until you can once again be present in the stillness and a nonjudgmental observer of your own and others' stories. Don't worry if this seems like hard work. It gets easier with practice. Savor the stillness when it does occur—even if it is fleeting. In that stillness, no matter how brief, know yourself to be a beloved child of God. That is your true story, and it rests in the quiet in your heart.

Yoga Poses—List of English/Sanskrit Names and Pose Focuses by Week

Common English Name	Traditional Sanskrit Name	Week
Airplane	*Virabhadrasana III* (variation)	38
Boat	*Navasana*	30
Bow	*Dhanurasana*	17
Bridge	*Setu Bandha Sarvangasana*	40
Butterfly (supine)	*Supta Baddha Konasana*	39
Camel	*Ustrasana*	21
Child's	*Balasana*	52
Corpse	*Savasana*	32
Cow Face	*Gomukhasana*	20
Dancer	*Natarajasana*	18
Down Dog	*Adho Mukha Svanasana*	22
Eagle	*Garudasana*	50
Easy	*Sukhasana*	8,48
Extended Side Angle	*Utthita Parsvakonasana*	26
Five-Pointed Star	*Trikonasana* (variation)	42
Forward Fold (seated)	*Paschimottanasana*	43
Forward Fold (standing)	*Uttanasana*	15
Hand Pose	*Mudra*	11
Hand to Foot	*Utthita Hasta Padangusthasana*	19
Hero	*Virasana*	7,8
Humble Warrior	*Baddha Virabhadrasana*	9

Common English Name	Traditional Sanskrit Name	Week
Knees to Chest	Apanasana	1
Legs Up the Wall	Viparita Karani	3
Lion's Breath	Simhasana	5
Locust	Salabhasana	49
Mountain	Tadasana	36
Plank	Phalakasana	16
Plough	Halasana	28
Prayer	Anjali Mudra	47
Reverse Prayer	Pashchima Namaskarasana	12
Reverse Warrior	Viparita Virabhadrasana	4
Side Plank	Vasisthasana	25
Sun Salutation	Surya Namaskara	45
Sunflower	Utkata Konasana (variation)	44
Tree	Vrksasana	14,38,41
Triangle	Trikonasana	23
Twist	Matsyendrasana	33
Warrior I	Virabhadrasana I	37
Warrior II	Virabhadrasana II	13
Warrior III	Virabhadrasana III	38

APPENDIX B

Practices Listed Alphabetically by Week, Pose Focus, and Scripture

Week	Practice	Pose Focus	Scripture
44	Abundance	Sunflower	John 2:1
49	Authentic Attitude	Locust	Isa 2:3
27	Be a Blessing	Random Kindness	Heb 13:17
4	Being Light	Reverse Warrior	1 John 1:7
16	Being Whole	Plank	Eph 2:8
17	Blessedness	Bow	Matt 5:8
24	Breathing Through	Slow Exhalation	2 Tim 1:3
6	Clear Vision	Eye Clock	Isa 42:5, 7
46	Coming Home	Steadiness and Ease	John 14:23
29	Community	On and Off Mat	Heb 10:24
37	Decluttering	Warrior I	Mic 6:8
40	Ditches	Bridge	John 14:6
38	Failure	Transition Balance	Matt 14:29
1	Freshening Up	Knees to Chest	2 Cor 4:16
8	God Whispers	Meditation Seat	Kgs 19:11–12
48	Gratitude	Easy	Psa 65:4b
41	Grounded	Tree	1 Chr 16:33
33	Happy and Holy	Twist	Rom 12:12
14	Healing	Tree	Rev 22:2–3
32	Healthy Self Love	Corpse	Prov 4:23
31	Holy Breathing	Three Breaths	Dan 10:17

Week	Practice	Pose Focus	Scripture
52	Hush	Child's	Psa 46:10
28	I Don't Know	Plough	Eph 3:10
30	Imperfection	Boat	John 2:5
43	Instilled Peace	Forward Fold (seated)	1 Cor 14:13
7	Inward Journey	Hero	2 Cor 4:16
18	Liberation	Dancer	Luke 13:12–13
3	Listen to the Soul	Legs Up the Wall	Psa 19:7
34	Longing and Belonging	Community	2 Cor 5:17
21	Managing Fear	Camel	1 John 4:18
5	Masks	Lion's Breath	Exod 34:29–35
12	Mystery	Reverse Prayer	1 Cor 15:51
13	New Day	Warrior II	Ezra 10:4
20	One Language	Cow Face	Acts 2:1
11	Open Hands	Hand Pose	Psa 63:4
10	Open Hearts	Fountain Breath	Eph 1:18
50	Patient Waiting	Eagle	Isa 40:31
19	Pause Button	Hand to Foot	Psa 46:1-3
42	Pilgrimage	Five-Point Star	Prov 3:6
45	Praise	Sun Salutation	Psa 145:3
51	Radiating Love	Candle Meditation	Eph 4:1
39	Restoring	Butterfly (Supine)	2 Cor 13:9
36	Returning	Mountain	Isa 30:15
2	Road Less Traveled	Favorite	Matt 2:12
47	Say Grace	Prayer	Rom 14:6
35	Showing Up	Balance	John 14:2–3
22	Slowing Down	Down Dog	Psa 23:3
15	Spirit Satisfaction	Forward Fold (stand)	Matt 6:33
26	Sustainability	Extended Side Angle	Psa 54:4
25	Third Way	Side Plank	Matt 5:43
23	Three Things	Triangle	Eccl 4:12
9	Walking With	Humble Warrior	Mic 6:8

Coordinating Devotions
to a Liturgical Calendar/Holy Week

We encourage you to coordinate your devotional yoga practice to your liturgical calendar if this adds meaning for you. We used the Revised Common Lectionary (1992), Year C, to inform the Scripture selections for each practice. However, because of the variability of Easter, our practices may not line up directly with your church liturgical calendar, particularly if you are currently in Year A or B of the Revised Common Lectionary, or if your church does not follow the lectionary. A practice for Holy Week is also included, below. Please see the Yogadevotion.com website for additional devotions corresponding to the current week and lectionary.

	Weeks	Devotion Themes
Epiphany	1–8	Light
Lent	9–13	Wandering
Easter	14–19	Healing/Renewal
Pentecost/Ordinary Time	20–46	Into the World
Advent	47–50	Preparation
Christmas	51–52	Wonder

The Practice of Entering the Easter Story
and Experiencing the Passion

This devotion is structured a little differently. Find a comfortable seat with your spine supported, and practice your opening breath work. Then read the four Scripture passages below, two times daily, taking time between the readings to locate yourself in the Holy Week story. The Scriptures include Palm Sunday, Spy Wednesday, Holy Thursday and close with Good Friday.

On Holy Saturday, consider taking part in an Easter vigil service, or you may find the following practices meaningful: the Practice of Mystery (Week 12) or the Practice of Managing Fear (Week 21). If you would like an Easter Day practice, consider the Practice of a New Day (Week 13) or the Practice of Being Made Whole (Week 16).

Begin the Passion Practice by asking the Holy Spirit to guide you into the Holy Week story in a new way. Ask the Spirit to help you experience the passion of Jesus, an exercise that grounds us in our faith and frees us to live as Easter people.

Palm Sunday: Reflect on this different kind of king.

> The disciples went and did as Jesus had directed them; they brought the donkey and the colt, and put their cloaks on them, and he sat on them. A very large crowd spread their cloaks on the road, and others cut branches from the trees and spread them on the road. The crowds that went ahead of him and that followed were shouting.
>
> "Hosanna to the Son of David!
> Blessed is the one who comes in the name of the Lord!
> Hosanna in the highest heaven!"
>
> Matthew 21:6–9

Spy Wednesday: Reflect on our own daily struggles.

> Then one of the twelve, who was called Judas Iscariot, went to the chief priests and said, "What will you give me if I betray [Jesus] to you?" They paid him thirty pieces of silver. And from that moment he began to look for an opportunity to betray him.
>
> Matthew 26:14–16

Holy Thursday: Reflect on Jesus' demonstration of love: slave to none, free to serve.

> Now before the festival of the Passover, Jesus knew that his hour had come to depart from this world and go to the Father. Having loved his own who were in the world, he loved them to the end. The devil had already put it into the heart of Judas son of Simon Iscariot to betray him. And during supper Jesus, knowing that the Father had given all things into his hands, and that he had come from God and was going to God, got up from the table, took off his outer robe, and tied a towel around himself. Then he poured water into a basin and began to wash the disciples' feet and to wipe them with the towel that was tied around him.
>
> John 13:1–5

Good Friday: Reflect on suffering and healing. (To be read in three parts.)

The place of betrayal . . .

After Jesus had spoken these words, he went out with his disciples across the Kidron valley to a place where there was a garden [to pray.]

The trial outcome . . .

So Jesus came out, wearing the crown of thorns and the purple robe. Pilate said to them, "Here is the man!" When the chief priests and the police saw him, they shouted, "Crucify him! Crucify him!

The cross . . .

So they put a sponge full of the wine on a branch of hyssop and held it to his mouth. When Jesus had received the wine, he said, "It is finished." Then he bowed his head and gave up his spirit.

John 18:1; 19:5, 29–30

Bibliography and Additional Resources

Useful Websites/Video:

Yoga Journal's Online Pose Index
  http://www.yogajournal.com/category/poses

Yoga Journey Productions (chair, gentle, and therapeutic yoga videos)
  https://www.youtube.com/user/YogaJP/videos

Christians Practicing Yoga Network
  http://www.christianspracticingyoga.com

Additional Devotions & Classes
  http://www.yogadevotion.com

Some of the Books That Have Inspired Us:

Adele, Deborah, *The Yamas and Niyamas: Exploring Yoga's Ethical Practice*
  (Duluth, MN: On-Word Bound Books, 2009)

Baptiste, Baron, *Journey into Power*
  (New York, NY: Fireside, Simon & Schuster, 2002)

Benson, Herbert, *Timeless Healing: The Power and Biology of Belief*
  (New York, NY: Fireside, Simon & Schuster, 1996)

Bourgeault, Cynthia, *Chanting the Psalms*
  (Boston, MA: New Seeds Books, 2006)

Brown, Brené, *Rising Strong*
  (New York, NY: Spiegel & Grau, 2015)

Devi, Niscala Joy, *The Healing Path of Yoga*
  (New York, NY: Three Rivers Press, 2000)

Dossey, Larry, *Healing Words: The Power of Prayer and the Practice of Medicine*
(New York, NY: Harper Collins, 1995)

Dossey, Larry, *Prayer is Good Medicine*
(New York, NY: Harper Collins, 1996)

Finley, James, *The Contemplative Heart*
(Notre Dame, IN: Sorin Books, 2000)

Gates, Rolf, *Meditations from the Mat*
(New York, NY: Anchor Books, 2002)

Kabat-Zinn, Jon, *Full Catastrophe Living: Using the Wisdom of Your Body and Mind to Face Stress, Pain, and Illness*
(New York, NY: Delta, Bantam Dell Reissue, 2005)

Keating, Thomas, *Open Mind/Open Heart*
(New York, NY: Continuum International Publishing Reissue, 2006)

Kraftsow, Gary, *Yoga for Transformation: Ancient Teachings and Practices for Healing the Body, Mind, and Heart*
(New York, NY: Penquin Compass, 2002)

Lasater, Judith Hanson, *Relax and Renew: Restful Yoga for Stressful Times*
(Berkeley, CA: Rodmell Press, 2011)

McLaren, Brian, *We Make the Road by Walking: A Year-Long Quest for Spiritual Formation, Reorientation, and Activation*
(New York, NY: Jericho Books, 2014)

Mueller, Wayne, *Sabbath: Finding Rest, Renewal, and Delight in our Busy Lives*
(New York, NY: Bantam Books, Random House, 2000)

Nepo, Mark, *The Book of Awakening, Having the Life You Want by Being Present to the Life You Have*
(San Francisco, CA: Conari Press, 2000)

Paul, Russell, *Jesus and the Lotus, The Mystical Doorway between Christianity and Yogic Spirituality*
(Novato, CA: New World Library, 2009)

Postema, Don, *Catch Your Breath, God's Invitation to Sabbath Rest*
(Grand Rapids, MI: CRC Publications, 1997)

Rupp, Joyce, *The Cup of Our Life*
(Notre Dame, IN: Ave Maria Press, 2012)

Ryan, Thomas, *Prayer of Heart & Body: Meditation and Yoga as Christian Spiritual Practice*
(Mahwah, NJ: Paulist Press, 1995)

Ryan, Thomas, *Reclaiming the Body in Christian Spirituality*
(Mahwah, NJ: Paulist Press, 2005)

Schiffmann, Erich, *Yoga, the Spirit and Practice of Moving into Stillness*
(New York, NY: Pocket Books, Simon & Schuster, 1996)

Swami Satchindanada, *The Yoga Sutras of Patanjali*
(Yogaville, VA: Integral Yoga Publications, 2012)

Swami Satyananada Saraswati, *Yoga Nidra*
(Munger, Bihar, India: Yoga Publications Trust, 1998)

Wolsey, Roger, *Kissing Fish: Christianity for People Who Don't Like Christianity*
(Bloomington, IN: Xlibris, Corp., 2011)